THE
Magnolia

∼ NOVELLA FOUR ∼

NAOMI FINLEY

ISBN: 978-1-989165-19-5

Cover designer: Victoria Cooper Art
Website: www.facebook.com/VictoriaCooperArt

Editor: Scripta Word Services
Website: scripta-word-services.com

Reading Order for Series

Novels:
A Slave of the Shadows: Book One
A Guardian of Slaves: Book Two
A Whisper of War: Book Three (Coming Soon)

Novellas:
The Black Knight's Tune: Novella One
The Master of Ships: Novella Two
The Promise Between Us: Novella Three
The Fair Magnolia: Novella Four

Novels can be read alone or with the novella series. The author's shorter works are best read in the suggested order.

∽ CHAPTER ∽
One

Savannah, 1842

DARKNESS ENGULFED ME AS I LET THE CURRENT PULL me down. River water gripped my lungs and gurgled in my ears as I struggled to breathe. Ceasing the thrashing of my arms and legs— fighting against the human instinct to survive—I waited. Searching for the cure. The sweet, peaceful release that came with the finality of death.

Ten years had passed since they'd taken my daughter, Magnolia, from me while I stood chained and helpless. Her sweet voice chimed in my head, over and over, like the striking of a blacksmith's anvil.

"Papa, I want to stay wid you. Please, Papa, I be good."

Each colored I'd come across, I'd described my girl and had received the same daunting answer: "Nah, never seed her." Then a reply from a grizzled woman lagging behind a gang of shackled folks headed to auction fueled my despair. "She jus' a face amongst thousands." The emptiness in her statement echoed the hopelessness dwelling in me, but I had continued to inquire until asking hurt more than living. And living…it had become worse than dying. Life held no purpose. No hope. Seasons had given me ample time to reflect on what had happened to my daughter, consuming me until the chains of slavery were twine in comparison to my inability to save her. I was property: an animal, a slave, a black man—powerless.

Let me die! Make et all end, I pleaded as the lack of oxygen ripped through my chest and skull.

Water splashed around me. Muffled voices shattered the darkness as hands grabbed me, hauling me to the surface. I coughed and puked up river water. The fogginess in my brain didn't clog my recognition of the masa's voice.

"Damn nigger!"

"What you fixing to do with him?" the masa's brother asked.

"Sell the bastard. It's time he becomes someone else's problem. No sense of survival in this one. Even the beasts of the fields have the desire to live."

"Been nothing but a problem since you purchased him."

"Well, that ends tomorrow. We'll throw him in the pit, and in the morning I'll take a trip into town and rid myself of him before there's nothing left to sell," Masa said. "Tie him up and let's get him on a horse."

Bound and sprawled across the back of the masa's mount, I withstood the half-mile ride to the masa's homestead. Reaching the farm, he reined to a stop outside the barn and twisted in his saddle before giving me a shove. I hit the ground with a bone-jarring thump. I lay unmoving, staring at the blue sky as the clouds drifted by.

Again, the One folks called God had forsaken me. When my girl Mag was bound in chains and led away, I'd cursed Him. I cursed Him for the injustice to my people, for taking my family, and most of all for giving me life. Somehow I'd become the reaper of the curse, never finding deliverance from my torment.

"Help me get him in the pit," Masa said.

They threw me into the hole, and I groaned as my body struck the cool dirt at the bottom. The iron grate scraped into place above, and I twisted and looked up, shielding my eyes from the glaring afternoon sun. Above me, the men peered down.

"No food or water for him. A night in the pit will do him good. We wasted a good part of a workday tracking him down. I oughta hunt down the lying scoundrel who sold him to me and take the trouble we've endured out of his hide." Masa rained his tobacco juices down on me before walking off, leaving me to wallow in my misery.

I dug my bare feet into the earth, pushing myself up into a seated position, and rested my head back against the dirt wall. Tomorrow I'd be auctioned for the fifth time in the years since I was sold from the plantation in North Carolina, where I'd lived with my family. Each masa was no different than the last. Like a mule I toiled in their fields, tended the livestock, and wielded their irons. "Yes, masa" and "No, masa" had become my few statements. I formed no friends or personal attachments with the folks in the quarters because I had no intention of staying. Burying all feelings for human life, I'd discovered a glimmer of contentment in caring for the four-legged beasts of the masas. I kept my head low, plotting and scheming about securing my freedom. I devoured my rations and built my stamina with one goal in mind: find my girl.

Mag had been sold to someone in Virginia, and I'd spent years trying to get there. Being hunted down by bloodhounds and dragged back to face punishment didn't stop me. But no purchase or escape had brought me any closer to Virginia or my girl, and it had left my body broken and my soul depleted. The realization of how big the world was off a plantation became daunting, and the dream of ever locating Mag withered. The urge to rescue my girl had been replaced with the wish that she no longer drew breath. Because being born colored only ensured suffering and loss. With my hope snuffed out, I was a slave without fear and with no will to live; I became a threat and financial risk to my masas.

I eyed each rock and root embedded in the soil of my current confinement with familiarity, pausing on the stick image carved into a large stone. Tenderly, I traced the eyes and face of the etching that had occupied the lonely hours spent in the pit. "Your pappy be a weak man. Ain't got et in me to fight no more."

Night fell, and I lay staring through the iron bars covering the hole in the ground at the star-speckled sky, ignoring the hunger gnawing behind my ribs and the thirst thickening my tongue.

"You awake?" a woman called from above.

I scrambled to sit up. "Yessum."

The grate scraped as she skidded it away, and I heard a light thump as something hit the ground in the far corner of the pit. I crawled toward it, fumbling about until I felt the rough cloth of a burlap sack. Opening it, I poked around inside, my fingers closing on a hunk of bread and then a slab of smoked meat.

She lifted her lantern and whispered down, "Eat up. Today you live. Tomorrow you can think about ending your life."

Giving in to her plea and the hunger knocking on my ribs, I shoved food into my mouth, choking with the urgent need to gorge on my first meal in days. Starvation wasn't part of my means to an end; it took more time than I could grant.

"Here, take this," she said. I looked up as she lowered a pitcher, and when I held it within my grasp, I drained the contents.

"Hurry up! They're passed out from drink but could awake at any moment. And it'll be the end of us both if I'm caught helping you."

I swallowed the food that felt lodged in the center of my chest, lifted the pitcher, and tried to get the last few drops of liquid. I coughed, the food slid down, and I placed the sack in the pitcher and gave the rope a light tug.

She reeled the rope in and without another word

moved the grate back into place. Rocking onto my knees in the swell of moonlight pouring into the pit, I listened until her footsteps faded.

Tomorrow the sun would rise, and another day would stretch, bringing with it the promise of an end to it all. And in this, I found some comfort.

CHAPTER
Two

E ARLY THE FOLLOWING MORNING, I WAS PULLED FROM the pit. Chained in ankle and wrist shackles, I awaited the masa in the front yard. Devoid of emotion, I stood with my gaze pinned on the sprawling field of unharvested cotton until a hummingbird flitting among the wildflowers freckling the overgrowth engulfing the house and dilapidated barn drew my attention. I studied the bird and considered the power within its rapidly beating wings. There was a time I had yearned to soar with the critters of the sky, to secure my freedom, but now I sought a different kind of liberty.

The masa entered the yard with rope, and I turned, held out my hands, and stood with my feet hip-width apart. As he looped the line through my shackles, I pondered on what my next masa would be like and came up with the same conclusion as before. Nothing a new masa would inflict on me would end my need to be free. Folks said there was no redemption for a man who took his own life, but I cared not. Because nothingness was the poison, I thirsted for it more than newborns fought to take their first breath.

The pregnant missus stood wearily by with a babe

balanced on her hip and her young son stationed at her side.

"I'll be back before dark," Masa said.

"Maybe you can trade him for a girl to help me with the children. She'd be company for me," she said.

Masa snorted with a shake of his head and turned to his brother. "And here I thought by getting myself a wife from the West, I'd secure myself a woman with some grit to her. I oughta send her back to her pa and ask for the younger sister. She sure was a heap more pretty than this sow." The men laughed, and the missus flushed, dropping her gaze. She wasn't a handsome woman, but she was mighty in spirit, a characteristic a person needed to survive when bound to a life of isolation. And the masa had ensured his wife found no ease from the loneliness embedded in her blue eyes for the family she'd left in the place called the West.

In the months I'd lived at the farm, I witnessed the disregard Masa held for his wife. She often became the butt of mockery from Masa and his brother, and if I was in the feeling business I might have been troubled over the abuse and ridicule she experienced. I had no room in the bitterness churning in my soul for anyone, though, let alone a missus. I'd made that mistake once, and it'd earned me nothing except the masa's wrath, and in the end it had cost me my girl.

Mounted on his horse, the masa gave instructions for his brother while he was gone. Then he heeled his horse into a canter, and I was forced to run to keep up or tumble to the ground and be dragged behind his horse. I wouldn't give the brothers the pleasure of seeing me fall.

Only when the farm was out of sight did the masa slow his horse in a trot. Winded, I tried to catch my breath, licking the dust from my lips.

"Water," I croaked.

No reply came.

"Water," I said again.

Masa jerked the rope tied to the horn of his saddle, nearly yanking me from my feet, but I managed to remain upright. His guffaw cracked above the rattling from my chains and the horse's hooves clipping the road.

Later, as the outskirts of the town grew in the distance, we encountered a well-dressed white man on a remarkable dark-coated steed with a blond mane and tail. "Good day, sir," he said to my masa before his eyes fell on me. "Headed to auction?"

I held his gaze; his brow pinched at my refusal to lower my head. I waited for his criticism of my masa for allowing his slave to brazenly stare at him.

"Who's asking?" Masa grunted.

The man broke from his inspection of me to turn his attention back to my masa. "Charles Hendricks. I'm a planter from Charleston. I'm in town on business."

"Hendricks?" Masa rolled the name over in his head. "Ain't you a captain or something?"

"No, but you may have seen my ships docked in the harbor."

Masa straightened in his saddle as it became

apparent the fellow was someone of importance. "I seem to recall your company name stamped on goods in town."

"That is a fact." He nodded in my direction and edged his horse closer. I dropped my gaze, but he reached out his riding crop and lifted my chin. Looking me square in the eye, he said to my masa, "You looking to sell him?"

"As quick as I can. Ain't nothing but trouble, this one. Got a death wish I can't seem to beat out of him."

"How much do you want for him?"

"Why? You looking to buy?"

The stranger sat, controlling my chin, forcing me to look at him. There was a familiarity in his gaze, an ache so vast it never seemed to fully heal. He released me and guided his mount backward. "Perhaps. I'm always in the market for strong, capable slaves. I've plenty of land that needs tending." Indifferently, he picked at the seam of his leather riding gloves.

"Ain't you heard anything I said? He's a brute of a slave, but he ain't nothing but trouble, sure to run off any chance he gets. And if you're hoping to get yourself a breeder, he ain't no good. His last owner said he can't get his business working, if you know what I mean."

Inside, I winced at the memory of the various girls and young women that Masa had brought to me. The desire for the closeness of another human had died in me long ago. No threats of the masa's dismembering my manhood had coaxed me. Naked, a knife to my groin, I had gritted my teeth with the agony of the first slash, refusing to cry out, and stared hard into the masa's eyes. His face had contorted, and then he assured me that "when I came to my senses" I'd never find pleasure in the warmth of a woman's bed again. His words had fallen on deaf ears because there was nothing left of me to break. I was already dead—a prisoner in a corpse that wouldn't die.

Mr. Hendricks craned his neck, eyeing me up. Masa stirred nervously on his horse.

"I'll pay you double the price you seek," the man said.

Masa inhaled sharply, greed rising in him. Then real slow like, he said, "I ain't looking to sell you damaged goods, only to have you come looking to settle a debt later."

Mister's jaw fixed. "I'll offer you triple the price and my promise as a gentleman that what deal we make to-day won't come back to haunt you."

"Why would you pay triple the price for a slave you'd have to hire a handful of overseers to keep an eye on?" He squinted at the man through heavy lids.

A peal of unnerving laughter tumbled from Mr. Hendricks. "I plan to break him."

Masa smirked. "Good luck with that." He chewed on the proposal a while longer before he thrust out his hand. "I'll take your offer. But remember, I warned you."

"Very well, then." He ignored the masa's out-stretched hand and tugged on the wrists of his gloves; his gaze held a callous glint. "Take him to the docks and ask for Captain Gillies. Tell him I sent you. He will pay you." He went on to inform Masa where he would find the captain.

"How's he going to know the deal we struck?"

"You're concerned he'll suspect you of robbing me?"

"Well, I…" Masa's face flushed red.

"Give him a message from me, and he will know the price was agreed on."

"What message?"

"*Change has come.*"

Masa's brow furrowed. "What kind of message is that?"

"You need not worry. He will understand."

Masa pushed the wad of tobacco wedged in his mouth with his tongue, then said, "I reckon I'll go find this captain of yours."

Mister tipped his hat, heeled his horse, and took off in the direction we'd come.

Masa uttered something inaudible under his breath before a gloating smile broke across his round, ruddy face. "Consider yourself taken." He spat in the dirt at the back of the stranger, then, whistling, he continued toward town.

CHAPTER
Three

MASA DISMOUNTED AND WALKED HIS HORSE DOWN the pier in search of the captain. He stopped in front of a warehouse and asked a man hoisting a crate on his shoulders about the Gillies man.

"Captain's down at the customs office signing the Warehouse Withdraw papers and settling duties. If you wait here, he should return shortly."

Masa nodded and mumbled his annoyance. "You." He turned to me, pointing at an empty space against the warehouse wall. "Sit."

I lowered myself to the ground, welcoming the chance to be off my feet. Thistles had embedded themselves in the soles of my feet and rocks had cut them during the journey to town. One by one, I picked out the sharp spines.

Masa positioned himself on the ground beside me to wait. Lowering his hat over his face, he gave the rope securing my shackles a yank. "Don't try anything stupid."

Soon his snores rose, and I took in the scene surrounding me. Through the hordes of workers and passengers scurrying about the docks, I watched barges loaded with bales of cotton and wooden crates sail up and down the Savannah River.

A wagon loaded with goods caught my attention as it moved toward us at a speed that had people leaping aside to avoid being trampled. The rotation of the wheels and the clomping of the horses' hooves beckoned me to take fate into my own hands. A quick dart into the path of the oncoming wagon would—

"I hear you're looking for me." A man's gruff voice snapped my head up and stirred the masa awake. Standing over us was a shorter fellow with hair the color of the flames in the belly of a forge.

"You Captain Gillies?" Masa clambered to his feet.

"Aye, I be him."

Masa reached down and seized me by the collar. "Up with you."

I obeyed and stood in the shadow of my masa.

"This slave is now the property of Charles Hendricks. He said I'd find you here and you'd pay me what is owed."

The captain folded his arms across his chest, not the least bit intimidated by the masa's bulk looming over him. "Is that so? And why do you think I'd believe he purchased this man without him here to say so?"

"He told me to relay a message: 'Change has come.'"

"Aye, I see. And tell me, what price did you agree on?"

Masa rumbled off the price, and the captain sputtered. "Outrageous. You're a bloody thief! I'll give you no such price."

"Are you in the business of purchasing slaves or not?" Masa's bellow turned the heads of passersby.

The captain gathered his composure, but his bite lay within his eyes. "Calm yourself, sir."

"Your boss set his eyes on my slave, and he was the one to set the price. Either you pay up, or I'll take the slave and sell him as I intended before Mr. Hendricks stopped us on our way into town."

Gillies's mouth twitched, and he turned to look at me. "Does your masa speak the truth?"

I eyed the masa's fingers, clenching and unclenching at his side, and remained quiet.

"He ain't much of a talker," Masa said. "Besides, what do you care what a nigger says anyhow?"

"I'll take my chances with him, as I believe there's more of a chance of him telling me the truth than you. Unless, of course, his desire to be rid of you outweighs his honesty."

"Only place he wants to be is in the ground," the masa muttered under his breath. Gillies never blinked.

I gasped as Masa elbowed me in the gut. "Well, speak up, you damn fool. Tell the man the truth."

Quelling the nerves snatching at my tongue, I obliged. "E-et be true."

"You wouldn't just be appeasing your masa, would you?"

"No, sah."

He studied me for a brow-sweating moment. "All right, I'll take the man's word," the captain said. "I'll fetch your payment. Wait here 'til I return."

As promised, he returned and paid the masa, who grinned, mighty proud of himself. He and his brother would celebrate tonight, and the missus would become the prize in their drunkenness. Fortunately for her, the babe she carried in her belly would keep her from bearing another child, unsure which man was the father.

Charles Hendricks returned to the docks, and soon the crew sailed his vessel into the Atlantic Ocean, and Savannah became a speck on the horizon. Waves lapped the sides of the ship as it pushed on toward Charleston—a place where I'd been held for a week in the slave pens before I was auctioned off.

The vastness of the ocean captured me, the salty breeze prickling my flesh. Closing my eyes, I inhaled deeply, finding pleasure in the ocean's mist on my face. For a moment a strange sense of peace washed over me as I listened to the squawks of the seagulls overhead and the calls of the crew. The accidental jab of an elbow from behind pulled me from my serenity. A black sailor mumbled an apology before he scurried off to perform his assigned task.

I stood unguarded at the railing, peering down at the water. It summoned me, and the ache inside of me listened. "I sorry," I whispered. The wind echoed my cowardice, skipping like a rock across the water. I placed my palms on the rail to hoist myself up.

"I'm in no mood for a swim today."

The gravelly voice halted me. I jerked and spun to find my new masa standing nearby, observing me. Freed from his frock coat and hat, he wore only a cotton shirt, dark trousers, and knee-high boots. In his hand he held a pair of shoes and bunched cloth. Without speaking he strode to the railing and rested his forearms on it, staring back the way we'd come. "I understand the desire to want to end one's life, but I ask you to consider a proposition I have for you," he said.

I stole a sideways glance at him.

"Are you willing to hear me out?" He focused on a bird gliding low across the water.

My shyness surfaced, as it had the first night Nellie let her shift fall to the floor and beckoned me with a finger, the peril of the masa's demand for us to breed balancing over us. I cleared my throat and tried to reply, but only a squeak came from me. "Yes, Masa," I managed to say.

"Good." He turned and gestured for me to take a seat on a crate. I did as instructed. The black sailor who'd ran into me earlier brought a bucket of steaming water and set it down on the deck beside the masa. The eagerness in his eyes to satisfy the masa was mystifying. "Good lad, now back to your duties."

Masa perched on a low crate in front of me. He set the shoes and rags down. "Give me your foot." He motioned with a hand. I hesitated. Impatience pulled at his face. "We don't need you getting an infection, or the steep price I paid to terminate your desire to die will be for naught."

His response only deepened my puzzlement. Why did a white man care 'bout a darkie wanting to kill himself? Especially one that hadn't been his property.

"Come now!" He slapped his knee.

Overcoming my uncertainty, I lifted my foot. He placed it on his knee before dipping the cloth in the bucket of water. He began washing the dirt and blood from my foot. I watched as he bathed my foot with a strange gentleness for a man of his color. "I do not know your story, and I'm not foolish enough to even begin to fathom what you have suffered. However, we may share a morsel of commonality. You see, there was a time in my life when I wanted to die more than anything. To end a pain so great, nothing else mattered—not even my daughter." He regarded me, and I swiftly dropped my gaze. The friendliness in his eyes heightened my suspicions of the peculiar white man. He didn't seem like a man to be easily misguided or fooled, so why would he allow my masa to cheat him?

He bandaged my foot, set it down, and took my other. "Do you care to hear more on the proposition I spoke of?"

My curiosity piqued, I nodded.

"Outside of Charleston sits the largest of my estates, where slaves and freed Negroes alike work my land. My daughter resides there, and when I'm away, she's left in the care of her mammy and servants. I've built a fortress around the child, handpicking each person with the hope that we can make a trade."

"Trade?"

"Yes. They care for what's mine, and in return, I provide them with shelter and as much freedom as I can allow—"

Freedom? What was he talking about? The only way a slave could taste freedom was to take it himself.

"I require men and women I can trust. And trust can't be earned by the lash of the whip now, can it?"

Again, my uncertainty mounted. "No, sah."

"Today I got an inkling about you when we met on the road. You have a fire in you—a passion, one may say—and I hope you'll find a way to harness such intensity and mold it into something worthwhile, perhaps of your own making. This country's crying out for good men and women to implement change. And change has come whether we're ready for it or not. Death is for the weak, and something tells me you're no coward. Whatever it is that feeds on your soul, I advise you use it to fuel a new perspective." He glanced at Captain Gillies, who stood directing orders to the crew. "A wise man once told me, 'Comes a time in life when you can't just exist. You got to start living. Got to do something that matters.' Thanks to that man, I can look at my own reflection without self-loathing. His wisdom and friendship have given me purpose and focus." His gaze drifted past me as he spoke, and he winced at some private thought. "Losses and discoveries in my life have set me on a path of change. We live in a world of prejudice, and I'm a man who has unleashed plenty of injustice not only on your people, but my own. I no longer wish to be such a man. If you give me a chance, you'll see you'll be treated with the fairness and decency a man deserves." He bandaged my foot, lifted the shoes, and held them out to me. "These look to be your size. Put them on."

It had been years since my feet had felt the leather of shoes. I reached for them and sat holding the shoes in my lap.

"I never got your name," he said.

"James, Masa."

He thrust out his hand. "I'm pleased to make your acquaintance."

I regarded him momentarily before clasping his outstretched hand. I felt the strength and steadiness in this white man's handshake. Sincerity permeated his intense gaze before a light smile tipped the corners of his mouth. Slapping his other hand over mine, he shook mine vigorously before rising to his feet. "Think on my proposition," he said, then turned and strode away, leaving me in a sea of confusion.

Who was Charles Hendricks, and what stoked his fierce passion?

CHAPTER
Four

I SAT ON THE FRONT SEAT OF A SUPPLY WAGON ALONGSIDE THE masa. He pointed to the left as the trees fringing the road gave away to fields of cotton bushes. "There she is, one of the most beautiful Sea Island cotton plantations around."

As we rode on, field hands straightened and rubbed at pangs in their lower backs, though they appeared, overall, to be robust and in good health. Some greeted the masa, who nodded in acknowledgment, while others sized me up. Two women smiled and tilted their heads together and whispered. My ears grew hot with the assumption they were wasting their excitement of new male prospects on me.

I looked past them to the big house that sat proud and gleaming beyond the fields. Its grand size announced the masa's wealth. Where my last masa's farmhouse had been crumbling at the seams, Masa Charles's stood winking at passersby.

"The crown jewel of the property, some say." The masa jutted his chin at the big house. "My wife took great pride in ensuring the home and surrounding grounds never lost their charm. Her presence seemed to fill all twenty-four thousand square feet of it, but now the home feels empty without her." Sadness weighted his words before he shook his head as if rejecting a memory. "However, Willow has enough spirit to keep all the house folk on their toes."

"She de missus?"

He chuckled lightly. "She likes to think she is. But no, Willow is my daughter."

Masa drove the wagon through the gates and down a lane canopied in scarlet and gold foliage of the ancient oaks. "Welcome to Livingston," he said.

At the back of the house, he reined the team to a stop. Outbuildings lined the perimeter of the work yard. Womenfolk walked past us supporting baskets of wet linens on their heads. A man balanced on a ladder, replacing charred exterior boards on a building. The smell of smoked meat wafted from the smokehouse. Young children, too tender for the fields, darted around men's legs and womenfolk's skirts, their giggles mingled with the sawing coming from the cooper and the clamor of the cotton gin.

"Papa!"

The shrill cry gripped my chest, and I searched for the owner of the youthful voice.

Masa Charles jumped down and moved around the horses to close the distance between him and the flash of yellow fabric and dark ringlets approaching. A child as pretty as the rising sun rushed at him. Masa bent with widespread arms to embrace her. His laughter thundered, and he rocked back on his heels as she launched herself at him.

"I missed you. You've been gone far too long," she said.

"My apologies, daughter. I returned as soon as possible. You must remember—"

She pulled back and regarded him with piercing green eyes. "Yes, yes, I know, 'I was always in your heart.'" Her mouth set obstinately, much like her pappy's.

"That's right." He tenderly struck her chin with a finger.

"I've been thinking. Next summer, I wish to stay here instead of staying in Charleston or making the long journey north. We've just arrived home, and I've missed everyone so. Besides, I've had to endure endless engagements with Lucille and the girls. They make fun of me, you know. They say that you leave me to be raised by slaves because you don't wish to father me. Lucille said I was practically a nigger." Tears formed in her eyes. "I told them it simply wasn't true. You do want to be with me, don't you, Papa?"

"Of course, but you know our livelihood depends on my business obligations afar. You hold your head up and disregard the gibbering of little girls. You're a Hendricks. Don't forget that."

"We're barely little girls," she said.

"What are you? Six? Seven?"

"Ten!" Exasperation skipped across her face. "Due to be eleven in the spring."

"Oh, yes, how could I have forgotten. I suppose I'll have to find another girl to gift with the doll."

"A doll?" Her expression darkened. "But, Papa, I told you I'm too old for such things." She straightened with the intention of appearing grown.

For the first time, I observed the masa becoming flustered. "Forgive me. I guess I'd forgotten—"

"Don't you worry none, Masa. Miss Willow would be grateful for whatever her pappy brings her." A portly house servant standing a few feet from them moved to position herself at the young missus's side. "Ain't dat so, Miss Willow?" The look the woman bestowed on the child caused her to lower her head.

"Yes, Mammy."

"And what you got to say for yourself?" The woman jerked her head at Masa Charles.

"I'm sorry, Papa. Maybe you could remember for next time that I don't like dolls." She tilted her head, her upturned face hopeful.

The child's mammy rolled her eyes and shifted her face to the heavens. "Lard, help de chile," she mumbled.

"I don't think I'll soon forget," Masa Charles said. "Now, I need to see to these supplies."

"Et good to have you home, Masa," the woman said.

"It's good to be home, Henrietta. I trust my daughter hasn't been too much trouble." He encircled Miss Willow's shoulders with an arm. The girl scowled up at him at his remark.

"Miss Willow ain't no trouble at all," the house slave said.

"I find that hard to believe. With each year that passes, she acts more like the mistress of the house than a child."

"Ain't dat de truth. She half-grown, she thinks." The woman chuckled and bestowed a look of devotion and pride on the girl. I'd heard tell of house slaves loving their white masas, and I suppose I'd witnessed it a time or two in my life. However, I couldn't understand such sentiments. After all, their kind was what was wrong in this world.

I climbed down from the wagon, and all eyes turned to me. I removed the hat the masa had given me during our journey and knotted it in my hands. My throat thickened at their curious gazes.

"I'll tell you all about my journey at supper," Masa said to his daughter.

Miss Willow clasped her hands together, pleased with his promise.

"I see the rebuild of the kitchen house is coming along." Masa observed the repair of the scorched building I'd noticed on my arrival.

"Dey finished laying de brick for de hearth last week. I reckon I can cook you up some splendid meals now." Henrietta rolled her shoulders back, and a smile crinkled the corners of her eyes.

"I look forward to it," Masa said over his shoulder as he turned and strode toward me. "I'd like you both to meet James. He joins us from Georgia."

"Why does he look so sad?" Miss Willow said, peering up at me. Her captivating eyes held my gaze a moment too long before I released myself from their spell.

"You need not worry, I have faith James will find Livingston to be of his liking," Masa Charles said.

"Don't you worry, mister, you'll like this place. I'll come to visit you every day." The girl slipped her hand into mine, determination settling on her face. Taken aback, I jerked my hand from her grip. Nervousness stirred in me. I got the feeling she intended to stick to that promise.

"You'll do no such thing." Masa spoke with the same sharpness he'd used when he'd conversed with my former masa on the road into Savannah. Henrietta cast a worried look on the child but remained quiet. Tears welled in the child's eyes, but the masa didn't notice. "You'll stay near the big house and away from the quarters. Do you understand?" His voice trembled slightly.

"But Papa—"

Masa's hands clenched into fists at his sides. "Willow!"

"Yes, Papa." She curtsied and bowed her head, but as her pappy turned his back to start unloading the wagon, she peeked up at me and grinned, then turned on her heel and skipped to her mammy's side.

"You mind your pappy, chile. He knows what bes' for you," the servant said.

I hurried to help the menfolk who'd come to aid the masa in unpacking the wagon. A solemnness overshadowed the masa, and he mumbled some orders before marching up to the big house.

On my way back from delivering a crate to a small warehouse, I saw the masa and the woman, Henrietta, conversing on the back gallery. Their tones were hushed, their words inaudible, but the masa's pacing and obvious distress left me to wonder if they were discussing the child's earlier interaction with me.

The masa I'd seen on our journey to this place was a different man. He'd shown compassion with no prejudice. But this masa and his reaction over his daughter's disregard of her position as a masa's daughter led me to believe he was a man who wore many faces.

CHAPTER
Five

FTER DUSK THAT EVENING, WHEN WE CAME IN FROM the fields, I was shown to the cabin I'd share with the weaver woman and her family. She had herself a brood of sons, two young ones whose reflections mimicked each other and three other boys who were about grown and ready to take on families of their own. Her husband was cornstalk-thin, with a puckered-up face and eyes that followed your every movement. He didn't say much, but he hardly had room to, because his woman wasn't like the meek and conquered womenfolk of the masas. No, sah. In the cabin, she was the masa over the men, and they respected her. When she spoke they sat taller, and when her voice rose, they tucked in their ears and averted their eyes. I got the feeling, real quick, I'd best be doing the same if I planned to stay out of her line of vision when she came unhinged.

Returning after a dip in the river to wash away the sweat and grime of the day, I entered the cabin. I stood just inside the doorway, wiping my sweaty palms on my trousers as the prospect of settling in with yet another group of strangers overshadowed me.

"Come in and shut de door. We ain't gwine to harm you." She waved her hand. I closed the door and stood regarding the cypress-planked walls of the one-room cabin.

The lithe woman was light on her feet, but her voice commanded the attention of the menfolk as she set a pot of collard greens in the center of the table. "As you can see, I got my hands full wid dis lot and I don't need no more men to care for. I 'spect you to pull your weight 'round here and in return, I fix your meals. Understood?"

"Yessum," I said.

Famished and having not eaten since morning, I salivated as I looked at the pot. I recalled the small gardens situated behind each cabin, and the hogs and chickens that roamed the quarters. Although some plantations I'd lived on allowed their slaves gardens to supplement the rations from the masas, pigs and chickens were a rare luxury.

"Got to speak up ef you 'specting to be heard."

"Yessum," I said a little too loud.

"All right, den." She turned back to the hearth and removed the skillet of biscuits from the coals. "You gonna have to share a bed wid Clem here." She nudged her head at the son that had inherited his mama's slimness. He was at the stage between boyhood and manhood, all awkward and disproportioned, stray dark curls invading his chin and cheeks.

I inclined my head, not liking the idea a bit, but I wasn't a blind man, so like the other menfolk, I kept my head down and my objection to myself.

"Good 'nuf." She gestured to the bench at the table, hardly big enough to seat us all. "Now sit, and we eat."

We sat elbow to elbow, and the family chatted amongst themselves, giving up on engaging me in conversation. I listened—I was best at that. The father chuckled quietly at the musings of one of his youngest sons. As I sat listening, longing for my own family burrowed inside me, but I blocked the feeling out as swiftly as it came. Cramped up in tight quarters with family folk had a way of doing that to you, and the solitude of the pit beckoned me.

After supper was over, I excused myself, left the cabin, and slipped into the night, basking in the quiet that had settled over the plantation. I sauntered on toward the corral and, when it came into view, exhilaration rose in my chest as I beheld some of the most beautiful horses I'd ever seen. Leaning on the fence, I watched the animals.

A silver-gray stallion standing sixteen hands high trotted over to me. "Hello, ol' boy." I trailed my fingers over the length of his nose, ran my hands down the extent of his neck and scratched. He prodded me in the chest with his muzzle. Resting my forehead against his snout, I let the warmth of his closeness soothe me, closing my eyes. I felt the tautness in my neck and shoulders ease.

Lost in the tranquility of the beast, I didn't hear the child approach until she was balancing on the bottom rung of the fence next to me. I jumped back, startling my new friend, and he stomped before moving off.

"Do you like horses?" Miss Willow asked, looking out over the corral.

I swerved to glance at the big house, half expecting the child's mammy or Masa Charles to be on the heels of the girl, but the dim light of the gallery lanterns and the light spilling from inside the home revealed no one. I was alone with the child. Fear strummed in my chest. "W-what you doing here?"

"I saw you from the parlor window, and I thought I'd come to keep you company." She rested her arms on the fence, her flesh pale against the dark curtain of night. Barely taking a breath, she continued. "I had to wait until Mammy went upstairs to prepare my bath before I could come join you. Do you like horses, mister?" she asked again, adjusting her footing on the rung.

I tried to swallow the bushel of nerves congregating in my throat. "Yes," I whispered.

"Me too. I don't like to ride sidesaddle because I like to ride real fast, but Papa says it's not ladylike," she huffed and turned her head to look at me. "Sometimes, I wish I were a boy. Because I think a son would make Papa smile more."

I observed her in the moonlight, noting the sadness that captivated her young face. And the loneliness and yearning for her pappy's time.

"If he had a boy, he could take him on his ships with him. He could learn all about Papa's affairs and see the world." Her eyes lit up. "It'd be grand, don't you think?"

I didn't have the stomach for a life at sea. I suppose

a person could get used to it after a while, but I liked the feel of the earth under my feet.

"Do you ever wish you were a girl?"

"No." My reply came as a squeak.

You got to go 'fore someone accuses you of harming a white chile. Despite the void inside of me and the need to pluck it out, being labeled a nigger who had harmed a child wasn't the way I wanted to leave this earth.

Miss Willow's chatter continued. "I don't blame you."

"For what?"

"For not wanting to be a girl. I think girls have it worse. There are too many rules."

If there was one thing I'd figured out about the child from my first encounter with her, it was that she had a mind of her own.

"You bes' git gwine 'fore your pappy comes luking." I glanced back at the big house.

"Oh, he won't be looking for me. He was tired from his journey and went up to bed. Told Mammy to make sure I was quiet, as he didn't want to be disturbed. Papa said he purchased you in Georgia. Is that so?"

I heaved a sigh and graced her with a nod.

"Did you have a family in Georgia?"

"No." Tightness twisted in my chest at the mention of my family.

"That's good," she said. "'Cause you would miss them a lot, with them there and you here. I thought Papa may have separated you from them, and that's why you look so sad."

"Ain't sad."

"Then what is wrong with you?"

"Nothin'. Jus' don't lak people."

She frowned. "All people?"

"Most."

"Sometimes grown-ups can be annoying, but surely you like children?" Not skipping a beat, she said, "Even though I'm practically a grown-up, I promise not to be a bore like them. Then maybe you will like me? Mammy says—"

"Miss Willow!" A breathless shout came from behind us. My heart thundered, and Miss Willow's feet hit the ground, lickety-split.

We spun to find her mammy charging toward us with her hands swinging at her sides as if the motion gave her momentum to quicken her stride. The expression on her face had Miss Willow running to her side.

"I'm sorry, Mammy."

"You ain't a lick of sorry. You bes' git on up to de big house 'fore I tell your pappy you done run off on me." Authority rang in her deep voice.

"No, please, Mammy." Miss Willow clasped the woman's hands in hers. "I won't do it again."

"How many times you gonna keep saying dat?" She scowled down at the girl. "I tole you, when you make a promise you got to abide by et 'til de end."

"But you see," Miss Willow eyed me, "I was keeping my promise. I told mister here I was going to come to visit him every day, and I was doing as I said."

The woman's scowl slipped a hair, and she gasped

before stifling a laugh. Then growing serious, she said, "You can't pick and choose what promises you gonna keep. You got to keep all of dem…well, 'cept dis one. Your pappy don't want you hanging round de quarter folks, so you skedaddle, and I think 'bout not tellin' him what you bin up to. Now off wid you."

She started to run off, then stopped and swung back. "Good night, mister."

I lifted a hand in a half-wave.

The house slave and I watched in silence until Miss Willow had disappeared inside before she turned back to me. "She a good gal, but she stubborn. I see she got a notion in her head dat she gonna make you happy, and et bes' you send her on her way when she comes luking for you, you hear me?"

"Yessum. I want nothin' to do wid de chile. I tried to send her—" I sputtered under her keen stare and looked away.

"I believe you," she said. "You don't luk lak de problem kind. And ef Masa Charles set his sights on you and paid de price of three nigras, I guess he thinks you decent 'nuf."

I centered my gaze on her. Earlier I'd viewed her from a distance, but now that she stood before me, I realized there was something familiar about the woman.

Boldly, she returned my inspection, her brow puckered. "You luk familiar. Have we met 'fore?"

"I a field slave. I don't go mixing wid de house slaves."

"Dat didn't stop nobody 'fore. Say, you ever owned by a Masa Adams?"

"No."

"How 'bout Masa Kinley?" she said.

"No."

"What dey call you again?"

I shuffled my feet in the grass, wanting her to take her questions and leave. "Jimmy. Sometimes James."

"I Henrietta. Folks call me Rita. You ever passed through Charleston 'fore?"

"Long time ago. Spent a week in de pens 'til I was sold to a masa in Columbia."

"What year you sold to dat masa?"

"'Round '32, I be guessing," I said.

"Late winter of '32?" Miss Rita moved closer, the earnest gleam in her eyes puzzling.

"I suppose et was." I stepped back, needing to put space between the fearless woman and me.

"Anything you 'member 'bout dat time?"

"I don't lend much time to thinking—"

"You bes' start!" she said, getting the take-charge tone in her voice.

"Why et matter why I was?"

"You men!" she scoffed. "You recall a woman and a chile dat stay in dat pen wid ya?"

"Dere lots of folks in de pens. Ain't 'bout to 'member no faces—"

"Think hard."

I stopped and thought a moment, too afraid not to give the woman the answer she sought. "Now dat you mention et, dere was a mother chained to me. She was half skeered out of her skin. Her infant be 'bout a year old or so. A gal…I think." Miss Rita had a way about her that pulled the words from me.

"I knowed et! Lard be praised." She flew at me.

I stumbled back as her thick arms embraced me. I froze, my hands hanging limp at my sides as she thumped my back repeatedly, as if we were lost kin.

"Et me. Me and my gal." She released me and stepped back. "We were in dat pen wid you. You helped keep me and my gal together."

My mouth sagged open. "You de same woman?"

"Dat I be."

"And de babe, she be dat gal I seed wid de young missus?" Hope sprang up in me.

"Dat she be. My Mary Grace has bin wid me evvy day since Masa Charles and Missus…" Her voice faded. "Since de masa purchased me. He let me keep my gal in de big house wid me, so I could see her grow."

Envy burned in my gut. I'd yearned to savor such moments with my own girl: to smell the sweet comfort of her skin and hair and hear her laughter. To have her arms squeeze my neck as I laid her down on the pallet, her soft whisper tickling my ear with, "Sing to me, Papa."

I wasn't able to carry a tune, but the closeness I felt in those times with my daughter used to be the vision that anchored me. When there was no fight left in me, the hope of being reunited with Magnolia had been my strength. With each blow of the whip or cut from the masa's blade in their efforts to thwart my rebellion, I'd cling to the image of her angelic face in my mind. *I see you again*, I had sworn before gritting my teeth to bear the brunt of their punishments.

I shook my head, brushing the memories away, leaving them in the past where they belonged. I didn't think on my girl no more. As the seasons changed, I allowed the masas to carve out the revolt in me, taking with it my memories.

"Dat is good, Miss Rita," I said, forcing a small smile.

"You all right?"

"Bes' I can be, I suppose."

"You luked lak somepin' stole you away."

"Oh, et ain't nothin'. I real happy for you and your gal," I said in a long, drawn out breath. My mind shifted to other matters. "And Masa Charles—you lak him?"

"Reckon so. Why you asking?"

"I seed de way you and him behave earlier. Lak he trusts and respects you."

"Got to trust me. He leaves his most prized possession in my care when he off on his ships. Got no choice, wid no womenfolk in de family."

"Where de missus?"

"Gone," she said dryly.

"Why he not marry again or hire a white woman to live in?"

"You can't tell de heart who to love. Masa Charles still in love wid his wife. And et hardly proper to have an unmarried woman living wid him. Besides, I de gal's mammy. She knows me bes'.'"

"Don't make no sense."

"Et do to us." She was knee-high to a baby calf, and

she stretched to the extent of her height and looked me in the eye, real hard like. "Don't you be gitting involved in de masa's business, and you do all right here."

"Yessum." My older sister's scolding face flashed before me, the time she'd caught me spying on her and the carpenter's boy kissing behind the privy. She had a fire in her like Miss Rita, a spark our masa had soon snuffed out. I was ten then, about the age of Miss Willow, when the masa came looking for my sister to warm his bed. It was a Sunday morning. I had been coming back from fishing at the river, and my heart was bursting with pride. That night, I'd chase the hunger from my ma and sister's bellies. I couldn't wait to see the excitement on their faces when they saw the stick weighed down with my catch. I was the man of the family. And I was taking care of them as my pappy had asked as he rode out in the back of the wagon to auction.

As I reached the cabin, I'd heard the commotion and my ma's tearful voice. "Please, Masa, she jus' a gal. Take me. I a real woman."

My heart stopped.

Panic and fear filled my sister's voice. "Mama, help me!"

"Masa, I beg you, don't do dis," Mama had said.

Through the side window, I saw my sister pinned facedown on the table and the masa behind her. He did a thrusting movement, and my sister screamed. I'd seen my share of grown folk carrying on so, but usually it had been hot and sweaty, and the wailing didn't sound so terrifying. I knew my sister was in trouble. I dropped the fish and broke into a run. Thundering up the steps of the stoop and into the cabin, I'd charged at the masa, beating at him with my fist and screaming insanities at him. That had been the first time the whip had marred my flesh. Masa said he should kill me. And I knew he could have, because it was illegal for a slave to strike a white man. However, instead, he sold me to a plantation a few miles away. I never saw my family again. But through the buzzing of slave talk, I learned my sister had borne the masa two children, and my mama had died some years later of malaria.

"James!" Miss Rita said.

I shuttered and barred the memory. "What you saying?"

"I said, what dis I hear about you trying to do off wid yourself?" Her hand rested on her thickset hip, and her face was screwed up like she warn't the least bit happy with me.

I opened my mouth to speak, but she didn't wait for a reply.

"Don't let me hear no tellin' of you trying somepin' so foolish. Whatever de blackness is dat be tearing you up, fight et. Ef you kill yourself, you letting de ones dat harm you win. Not a day goes by dat I don't long for my Big John, and I suppose 'til I take my last breath I will love dat man. But I know he'd want me to live, not only for me, but for my gal."

"You got somepin' to live for," I said dryly.

"So do you. We all got our own journey to walk in dis life, and no one ever said et be easy. De path my footprints leave is different den yours, but I be damned ef I'm gonna let de white men write my story. De Almighty and I be in charge of dat. We slaves and et ain't right, but we survivors and we gots to fight. Ef you lost your way and reason to fight, you bes' be luking for a new reason to git up evvy morn." Tears misted her eyes. Turning away, she blotted her eyes with the hem of her apron. Without turning, she said, "Et good to see ya. I hope you give what I say some thought." With that, she ambled toward the house.

Left in the heaviness of her words, I strode to the fence and rested my elbows on the post. *Find a new reason.* I chewed on her words. She didn't know my story, and she still had her girl. The corners of my eyes dampened. I blinked through the blur, and the old anger I'd caged rushed in at the recollection of how Miss Rita had spoken of Nellie's God with affection. *Blacks and whites alike say there is a God. But where is He? I, for one, will never bow my head to Him because a God that tilts His favor on the pale faces is no God.* He allowed the whites to rule the sinking crypt we, with unyielding pride, called the United States of America. The injustice of this focus had kindled rage within me. And for years I'd spent my days in the fields dreaming of strangling my white masas in their beds to cleanse the earth of their abomination once and for all. I barely recognized the man I'd been back then. Empathy and compassion that had once thumped in my chest for all the living had shifted to bitterness and resentment.

The whites had lined their pocketbooks on the backs of slavery, divided our families, stole our children's virtue and childhoods, raped our women, and treated us worse than animals. If we stood up against our white masa, like a hound dog corners a rabbit and flushes him out, we were hunted, beaten, and murdered. They feasted on the fruit of their lands that came from our labor, while we died off like flies from various diseases, illnesses, and hunger. Lending emotion to the whites was something I could no longer muster. Hollowness had displaced the exhaustion of carrying pent-up rage, but within the bleakness now inside of me I existed in a fever that wouldn't break.

The burden of the dismal life I'd been given rested heavily on my shoulders as I turned on my heel and strode toward the cabin. Death's hand had once again outplayed me and for this night, I allowed it to win.

CHAPTER
Six

THE MOON'S ARM STRETCHED ACROSS THE CABIN floor from the single window, casting shadows from the figures behind the makeshift curtain. I lay on the pallet next to the weaver's son Clem, staring at the ceiling, waiting for the woman and her man's lovemaking to be over.

"Bes' git used to et," Clem whispered. "'Fore we come here, Ma and Daddy were too tired at night to cause a racket. Now wid Daddy managing folkses' rations and not so tired from long days in de fields, et become a nightly occurrence. Masa needs to put him back in de fields, so de rest of us git ourselves some sleep."

"When you come here?" I whispered back.

"'Bout six years ago. Not long after de masa did a cleansing of de place."

"What kind of cleansing?"

"Folkses say Masa sold most of de original slaves off after de missus disappeared. But dat was de fust cleansing."

"Dere was another?" I said.

"Yes. After de masa returned from across de ocean last winter, he slowly started dismissing his overseers and hired men, only to replace dem wid de ones dat run dis place now."

"Why he do somepin' lak dat for?" I said.

"Nobody knows. Ma says not to be prying into matters dat don't concern us."

His mama talked sense. It didn't matter if this new masa had shown me kindness, he was still a masa, and I was still a slave. I wasn't about to go caring about him or his family, regardless of his proposition.

"You lak dis place?" I said.

"Et all right for de most part. But as good as et might be here, et ain't free."

Soon the grunts and moans of the couple stopped and a hush settled over the cabin. I rolled onto my side, thinking on my Nellie. Sadness…it never came. Like the night sweats, it didn't visit me no more. I slept through to the morning, only waking to the coughing of one of the children.

After breakfast, I followed the family out to the work yard, where other workers had gathered. Two men sat upon horses. The man on the chestnut bay had flesh that the sun burned and mapped with a mass of freckles. He peered at us with watery brown eyes that flickered nervously.

I examined the rangy man on the pinto horse. Permanent grooves were etched into his jowls, suggesting the scowls of a none too friendly kind of fellow. As he stated the task for the day, Clem leaned close and said in a low voice, "Dat Jones. He de head overseer here now. His men and him showed up here a few months back wid de masa. Folkses say dey from Michigan."

Some years back, Michigan had joined the Union in becoming the twenty-sixth state. Around open fires in the quarters, after a day's work, I'd listened to hushed discussions about the number of abolitionists in the state who helped slaves get to freedom under a secret system they called the Underground Railroad. They said that one mile across a river from a place called Detroit lay the promised land of slaves' dreams. At one time, my head was filled with the same rubbish.

Jones heading south to secure work as an overseer was all the confirmation I needed—he was no different than all the rest. "Got a thirst for darkie blood, does he?" I said through clenched teeth.

Clem shrugged his narrow shoulders up to touch his big ol' floppy ears.

Jones had finished his instructions, and the crowd began to disperse. I hurried to fall into line, but the overseer's voice pulled me back.

"You," he said. "What is your name?"

I stopped in my tracks and turned reluctantly back. "James, sah."

"You're to work in the fields 'til Mr. Hendricks and I figure out where you'll best fit in."

I nodded.

"All right," he said, as though conversing wasn't something he was fond of and he didn't know what to say next. "Well…off with you, then."

I inclined my head, as eager as him to end the

awkwardness, and took off at a jog to catch up with the others.

When the lunch wagon came at high noon, Miss Willow sat on the front seat next to her pappy and the weaver woman's man. Masa jumped down and turned to lift Miss Willow to the ground, but she was already moving over the side of the wagon, using the wheel spokes to climb down.

Masa Charles's lips pressed tight, but the rebuke on the tip of his tongue he reserved. He went to assist the man, who had clambered over the seat into the bed of the wagon and started filling bowls with grub.

Miss Willow helped her pappy distribute water to the workers, and when she reached me, she smiled—a gesture that reached her eyes. "Morning, mister."

"Morning," I said, then drained the ladle of water before handing it back to her.

"You like it down at the weaver's cabin?"

I wondered how the child knew what cabin the masa had set me up in. "Et good."

She leaned in and cast a glance in her pappy's direction before whispering, "I was worried when I found out Papa had put you there." She straightened and said in an even tone, "I play with her twins sometimes, and they say their mama is downright scary. Once she whipped poor Simon with a switch until he couldn't sit down for a week." Her eyes narrowed with displeasure. "And all because he didn't say grace before he dug into his dinner."

Laughter cut through the mouth-smacking of

hungry workers, and I looked to see Clem grinning from ear to ear at the little missus's remark about his mama.

Masa overshadowed her. "Willow, move along."

The child glanced up at him, and the stern expression on his face halted her protest. Her lips quivered as she moved on down the line.

Masa turned to me. "I trust your first evening went well?" His grimace faded.

"Yes, sah."

"Good to hear. Tomorrow I require a driver. Please have the wagon ready and out front. We leave for town at first light."

I bowed my head. "Et be ready."

Before we returned to the fields, I saw Masa Charles speaking to Jones, who glanced in my direction and gave him a stern nod. I assumed I was the subject of the conversation.

Some time later, in the fields, Jones rode up to me. I straightened, my fingers clasping the hoe.

"Mr. Hendricks says you were a blacksmith."

"Yes, sah." I removed my hat and used my forearm to wipe the sweat from my brow.

"I need to pull you from the field and send you down to give Jabet a hand with shoeing the horses. His arthritis is acting up, and he is behind in his tasks."

At the blacksmith shop, I found a man with a full head of hair the color of cotton, pumping the leather bellows to regulate the temperature of the forge. He cocked a brow at me. "You de one dey calling Jimmy?"

"I be him."

"Come make yourself useful." He shuffled to a table where knives and other tools lay spread out. "Masa Charles wants dose blades sharped and returned to de big house."

My brow puckered. "Ain't he got plenty of house slaves for dat?"

"You thinking de masa don't know how to run his own household?"

"No, I—"

"Got no time to waste on answering questions. Bes' you do as you're tole and know your place. We don't put up wid no troublemakers 'round here. Now you do yourself good and git dose sharpened." He slapped the table and gave me the eyeball before ambling over to the anvil. He placed a metal piece into the crimson coals, and shot a look my way. He nudged his head at the table. "Whatcha waiting for? Git at et."

Damn plantation is infested wid uppity coloreds. I lifted a blade, turning it over in my hand, then ran my finger along it, pulling back my finger at the bite of the edge. I picked up another knife on the table and tested it. Most were hardly in need of sharpening. Nevertheless, I picked one up and started the assigned task.

It was when I laid the last tool down and stepped back that I noticed the masa watching from the shadows of the doorway at the far end of the shop. His face unreadable he turned, strode outside, and disappeared. I stared after him with the full realization he had tested me, seeing what I would do with the temptation he'd intentionally set before me.

I spent the next hour or two removing rust from horseshoes. The movement of the wire brush in my hand paused when voices from the back gallery drew my attention. From my position in the shop, I had an unobstructed view through the large window, its shutters thrown open, of Miss Rita, her daughter, and Miss Willow. Miss Rita stood tying the ribbons to the white girl's bonnet.

"Mind you stay away from de river." Miss Rita's voice carried. "De current is high and dangerous. No wandering off, you hear me?"

"Yes, Mammy," Miss Willow said.

The other child chimed behind her, "Yes, Mama."

"I mean et, Miss Willow, you gals go play in your castle and not a step farther."

In unison, the girls shook their heads, promising again to abide by her orders.

"Now off wid you. I got dinner to prepare. Mr. Bennick is coming, and your pappy will 'spect you clean and shiny for his guest."

"Don't you worry none," Miss Willow said as she made her descent down the steps with a basket hanging on the crook of her arm.

"As long you as you be 'round, I always have somepin' to worry 'bout," Miss Rita called after them before shaking her head and ambling back inside.

I blew on the loosened rust on a horseshoe and rubbed a cloth soaked in vinegar on the stubborn bits.

"I finished," I said.

Jabet hobbled over to inspect my work. "Dat will do. You know much 'bout horses?"

"Yes."

"Got a lame horse dat needs tending. Head on down to the river and fill dose buckets. Dere a trail down by de quarters de washer woman use. Can't miss et."

At the river, I moved to a shallow inlet and crouched to fill the buckets. Mesmerized, I watched the racing of the current farther out as it thrashed and swirled in its madness. My pulse galloped. I stood. My feet moved forward. I stepped into the water, and it charged at my ankles, filling my shoes. My time was now. I would take my chance. Let the river take—

"Miss Willow, be careful," Mary Grace said. Tears thickened her voice. "Mama said we aren't supposed to be down here."

I glanced around and spotted the girls through the brush extending out on the embankment. Miss Willow was walking the edge of the bank. She placed one foot in front of the other as she steadied her balance with her arms.

I stepped back onto the shore, water swishing in my shoes. *Blasted gal don't listen to nobody.* One of the weaver's switchings would do the child some good. I set the buckets down.

"Please, Miss Willow, come away from that edge," Mary Grace pleaded.

Keeping low, I proceeded along the bank, staying hidden behind the overgrowth.

"All right, let's sit," Miss Willow said, and the girls disappeared out of my line of sight.

Parting the overgrowth with a hand, I located the

girls, perched on a boulder with their heads close together. Mary Grace held an open book.

"Read this line, right here," Miss Willow said.

Mary Grace began reading, and the words effortlessly flowed from her, as if she had been studying for years.

"The word is *therefore*," Miss Willow said. Then she enunciated, pressing her tongue against her teeth to start, then breaking the word up. "TH-ERE-FORE. Therefore."

"Therefore," Mary Grace repeated.

"Good!" Miss Willow clapped her hands with enthusiasm. "You're so smart, Mary Grace. Smarter than Julia and the other girls."

The child beamed. "You think so?"

"Sure do. And if we keep on with your learning, you will grow up to be the first colored girl to ever read and write."

"The first one in the whole world?" Awestruck, the child let the book rest in her lap.

"Of course! Can you imagine if all the coloreds on this plantation learned to read and write? Wouldn't that be wonderful?"

"Ain't it dangerous?"

"*Isn't* it," Miss Willow corrected. "You know it is. But we are brave."

"I don't feel so brave."

"Nonsense." Miss Willow jutted her chin out. "We're only as brave as we believe we are." Then her shoulders slumped a little. "Well, that is what Papa says."

My foot slipped on a rock, sending a landslide of loose gravel and stones down the slope and alerting the girls of my presence. They jumped, and Miss Willow quickly grabbed the book from Mary Grace's lap and hid it under the folds of her skirts.

"Who's there?" Fear cracked Miss Willow's voice.

I cursed under my breath and stepped out with my hands lifted in a sign of peace. "Et jus' me, Miss Willie."

"Mister, you frightened us. What are you doing here?"

"Come to git water, Miss Willie."

"Willie?" Her brow puckered. "My name is Wil-low."

"Dat what I said." It was my turn to frown.

She shook her head. "No, you said, Willie."

"Ain't dat your name?"

Her brow eased and a smile grew on her face. "You can call me that."

As bright as Miss Willow appeared, her confusion over her own name left me scratching my head.

"Didn't your mama tell you not to be playing by the river?" I said to Mary Grace.

Miss Willow swallowed hard, her eyes big and round like.

"You bes' listen, don't ya think?" I glanced from one girl to the other.

The girls bobbed their heads like the trumpeter swans that glided on the pond out front.

"Ef someone catches you teaching dat gal to read," I gestured at Miss Rita's gal, "she be de one to suffer. You understand?"

Tears welled in Miss Willow's eyes. "We do," she said. "And I won't let anyone hurt Mary Grace. Ever!" The fierceness and determination on her face made me believe the girl.

Masa calling out her name alerted us all, and Miss Willow scrambled down from the rock like a slave does when he hears his masa's call. She grabbed her basket and tucked the book underneath the cloth concealing its contents. "Come, we got to go!" Taking Mary Grace's hand, she half dragged her as they pushed past me. "Have a good day, mister," Miss Willow shouted over her shoulder as they climbed the bank and disappeared.

Not wanting to be seen coming from the river with the children, I waited a few more minutes before I returned to the blacksmith's shop.

CHAPTER
Seven

THE NEXT MORNING I HAD THE CARRIAGE READY AND waiting out front of the big house when Masa stepped onto the front gallery. His manservant trailed behind him with the masa's top hat and a black frock coat. He held out the coat for Masa to slip into before handing him the hat.

"Thaddeus, please see to it that someone takes grain and oats to Mrs. Jenson. With her husband's recent passing, she isn't herself, as one should expect. Her servant, Ruth, said she'd taken to her room and was refusing guests. Ask Henrietta to prepare her a basket of other items she may need. It's our neighborly duty to keep watch on her until she gets back on her feet."

The colored man was fairer in complexion and carried himself with the grace and poise of a man far beyond his station. With a bowed head, he lightly placed a white-gloved hand to his heart. "I'll see a wagon is sent to the Widow." Thaddeus's speech was that of a refined colored.

From my position at the carriage stone, I peered at the man, wondering where the masa had purchased him. Men like him were often sired by a masa and given favored stations in the big house along with privileges withheld from the quarter folks.

Miss Willow burst out the open door with the ever obedient Mary Grace close behind. Both girls were clad in bonnets and capes. "We're ready, Papa," Miss Willow said, excitement dancing in her voice.

"Willow, you must learn to walk and not bounce around so. If you're to become a lady, you must start carrying yourself as such."

Her lightheartedness faded, and she stiffened. "Yes, Papa."

"Boarding school will do you some good."

She grabbed his arm, her face pinched. "But Papa, I don't want to leave Livingston. I love it here. And what will Mary Grace and Mammy do without me?"

"Rest!" he said with a snort. "Do not worry, you've got a few more years before you're old enough. But you *will* be going. And it's best you prepare yourself for it. Because when the time comes, I won't hear any fussing. Besides, I assure you, the teachers will be much harsher than I." He swerved back to his manservant.

Miss Willow stood unmoving, looking as though she'd break into tears at any moment. Mary Grace, who had stayed at her side, stroked the little missus's arm and whispered something to her. Miss Willow nodded, looking at the slave girl with a fixed smile.

A smart man or not, when it came to his daughter, Masa was a fool. Couldn't he see the admiration in her eyes when she looked upon him? Or the need for a little of his time? Why did he want her all grown? Stealing her childhood like the whites did our children warn't right.

What you care for, anyway? I veered my gaze to my new shoes. *I don't.* The shoes pinched my toes, but I didn't mind that much, 'cause they were mine.

"Come, Willow, if you insist on accompanying me to town, we need to be on our way." I looked up as the masa held out a hand to Miss Willow, who slipped her gloved one into his.

Peering up at him, she smiled, eager to please. "It will be a grand outing, Papa. You'll see." Her small shoulders squared, and her nose tipped up in similar fashion to her pappy's.

"Let us hope so." He gave her hand a tender squeeze as they descended the stairs, the slave child falling in line behind them.

"Wait!" Miss Rita rushed from the big house. She gathered the fabric of her skirt in her hands and pounded down the steps, hurrying after them.

"What is it, Henrietta?" Masa pivoted, impatience tightening his face.

Tears and panic glimmered in Miss Rita's pretty eyes. Years had rounded her body, and she warn't the curvy little thing I remembered, but she was still as beautiful as ever. "Please, don't let anything happen to her. Promise you keep her safe." She grabbed at the masa's hands.

I sucked back a breath and stepped forward, fear pounding in my chest. *No!*

But he didn't strike her or fall back, astonished and repulsed by her touch.

"Oh, for heaven's sakes," he said with a roll of his eyes. "We're going to town. What could possibly happen to the child?"

She released him and drew Mary Grace into her protective wing, squeezing her as though it may be the last time she laid eyes on the girl. "Lots," she said with surprising bluntness. "Keep her close."

"Yes, yes, of course. No need to worry. The child will be fine. Now," he said to Mary Grace, "in you go."

Sensing her masa's agitation, the child stumbled up the steps of the carriage stone, and instinctively, I reached for her. Miss Rita looked up at me, her taut expression softening, as if she found comfort in my accompanying them to town. Clearly spoiled by the masa and her years in the big house, her insight of stations had dulled. I couldn't save my own girl from the white plague. What made her think I could save hers if something went awry?

"Papa's right, Mammy," Miss Willow assured her. "You've nothing to worry about. Mary Grace and I will be together. Nothing can happen as long as we have each other."

Masa chewed on the side of his mouth and mumbled something under his breath before climbing the stone carriage steps and helping his daughter into the carriage. Miss Willow seated herself beside Mary Grace, but with a sharp look from her pappy, she moved herself to the other seat.

He climbed in and sat down beside his daughter. "Get us on our way, James," he said.

His dark mood had Miss Rita's girl crouching in the corner. Miss Willow folded her hands in her lap, extending her neck just so, and rolled back her shoulders, trying her best to appease her pappy with the posture of a lady much beyond her years. As I closed the door, through the gap in the curtains, I saw the masa reach out and pat her knee.

On the drive to town, I thought about the regrets Masa Charles would have in life, the missed opportunities with his daughter and the damage he unconsciously was inflicting on the girl. If I had one more day with my girl, I'd do things differently. I'd fight the weariness in my body and appreciate each moment because—in this life—there was no assurance.

Out front of the general store, I stood by the closed carriage door, waiting for the masa. Inside the buggy, Miss Willow and Mary Grace laughed and carried on in a way that was sure to displease the masa. Through the large window extending along the front of the store, I observed Masa Charles moving about the shop. Every so often he would pause and look at the merchandise, then the shopkeeper, who was occupied with a customer. But when the customer wasn't looking, she'd glance Masa's way.

Soon the store door opened and the fellow the shopkeeper had been tied up with left. Masa promptly set aside his interest in the store's merchandise and strode up to the shopkeeper, who moved from behind the counter to greet him. He shook her outstretched hand, and their grasp lingered.

Masa leaned close and spoke to her. She gaped at him and shook her head, then adjusted her spectacles before she replied, hands flailing. He spun away from her, removed his hat, and swiped a hand over his face; something she had said upset him.

Their gazes shifted to the window, and I dropped my gaze. After a moment I returned to observing the pair inside. Masa Charles turned away from the woman, and quickly she smoothed her bodice and patted at the sides of her blond, pinned-up hair—an indication of attraction I'd witnessed other women perform when they were interested in a fellow. If you listen and watch and do less talking, life finds a way of telling you the secrets folks strive to withhold. Though the shopkeeper could rival Masa Charles with her ever-present somber expression, she eyed the masa with a look that went beyond whatever business arrangement I assumed the pair had. However, Masa's businesslike manner never faltered. I'd come to understand in my few days with him that he was skilled at keeping folks, including his daughter, at a safe distance. His mastery unsettled me. I looked down at the straw hat I held, picking at the edges with my fingers.

The door of the shop squeaked open, and Masa and the shopkeeper walked onto the boardwalk.

"It isn't so!" Mary Grace said with a gasp.

"It is so. She eats children at luncheons." Miss Willow's response was muffled.

"Says who?"

"Lucille."

I twisted to find the girls with their noses pressed against the glass of the carriage window, their eyes looking past me toward the store. I followed their gazes.

"Hello, Mr. Hendricks." Two young fillies, around twenty years old or so and young enough to be Masa's daughters, giggled and swayed, taking themselves a good old gander of a handsome gentleman.

Masa tipped his hat. "Ladies," he said as a gentleman would, never dispensing interest in their dalliances.

The shopkeeper's permanent scowl deepened. "Move along, ladies. Can't you see Mr. Hendricks and I are engaged in business matters?"

The girls obliged her and moved down the boardwalk. Casting a glance over her shoulder, one muttered under her breath, "Northerner."

"As always, it's a pleasure doing business with you, Charles." The woman bestowed a modest smile on him.

"As with you, Miss Smith."

"See how she looks at him? Like he's a teacake she wants to devour," Miss Willow said, jealousy in her tone.

I ducked my head, stifling a chuckle. *Maybe she be de reason de masa never found himself a new wife.*

I opened the door, and the girls shuffled back to their seats as the masa entered the carriage. Climbing into the driver's seat, I flicked the reins, and we were on our way.

CHAPTER
Eight

O FTEN IN THE DAYS TO COME, M ASA C HARLES PULLED me from the fields to drive him into Charleston to deliver goods to his warehouses and ships. I accompanied him to neighboring farms and plantations to distribute products that had come in on his ships. I got the feeling it was his way of keeping me occupied, making me less of a risk to him and to myself.

The day of the accident, I'd been at Livingston for a few months and had returned to my position in the fields. A shrill scream rose above the workers' chanting melody. The woman next to me dropped to the ground clutching her face, blood oozing through her fingers and staining the front of her shirt. Beside me on the ground lay the metal end of the hoe that had broken away from the handle.

"Git de doc," I shouted, my feet rooted to the earth.

"I git him," a man said before running off.

A woman stooped beside her, wrapping an arm around her shoulders, whispering words of comfort.

The overseer's right-hand man nudged his horse through the crowd of concerned folks flocking around us. He dropped from his mount. My fingers clenched at my sides, and as I'd grown accustomed to, I stilled the need to help, keeping my distance and letting the overseer's man handle the situation. "What happened?" he said.

"De end came off de hoe," someone said.

He knelt beside the injured woman. "Carlota, let me see how bad it is."

Her sobs eased for a moment and she opened her hands. The hoe had slashed her from forehead to chin. Murmurs and gasps come from those gathered, and some of the womenfolks' hands shot up to cover their mouths; others turned their heads away. As he assessed the damage, his face paled, and he rocked back on his heels like he was about to faint. Carlota closed her hands and returned to applying pressure to her face.

"You." Gesturing to me, he rose to his feet. "Take her to meet the doc. Make it quick before she bleeds to death."

I forced my feet to move. Bending, I hoisted the bulky woman into my arms. The warmth and weight of her body against mine felt foreign and awkward. "Evvything be all right. Doc fix you right up," I said.

Her weeping fell to a whimper. With her hands still clasped over her face, she rested her head on my shoulder.

The overseer's man mounted his horse, then guided it back down the row and away from the blood pooling in the dirt and staining our clothing.

◈

After retrieving a new shirt from the cabin, I grabbed a bucket and filled it with water and went behind the barn. Hidden from view, I tossed the clean shirt in the grass and slipped out of the bloody shirt clinging to my flesh. I washed the red stain from my forearms and hands before ladling water over my neck, chest, and shoulders. Lifting the bucket, I poured the remainder over my face. In the sweltering afternoon and the heat pumping from my skin, the brief cooling effect of the water channeling over my body mimicked warm beads of sweat.

A gasp sounded behind me. I jumped and dropped the bucket, whirling to find Miss Willow standing a pebble toss away, her pretty face twisted with concern.

"Did your last master do that to you?"

Ignoring the girl, I darted for my clean shirt.

"I said—"

"I heard what you done said," I retorted, wiggling the shirt over my head.

"Well, did he?" She sauntered toward me, her gaze pinned on my scars.

Panic leaped in my chest at her closeness. I glanced around, looking for a way to escape the girl. In my days at Livingston, I'd come to see how the masa guarded the child with a fierceness that went beyond the affection and protection of a parent; instead, his ways with the girl seemed to be driven by some sort of strange obsession. From afar, I'd observed how he watched after her, almost afraid she would take a tumble and be left broken. When visitors arrived, Masa Charles's eyes immediately scoured the grounds looking for the girl, often instructing her mammy to usher her inside. His posture became rigid, his demeanor dry. He'd receive his neighbors and guests with the grace and respect of a Southern gentleman, but the greeting never passed beyond words and a feigned cheerfulness.

"Mister, you gonna answer me?" Miss Willow said.

Each time she addressed me as mister, it left me stunned and lost for words. Her word choice was a courtesy never bestowed on a slave. Nevertheless, it didn't divert me from the need to be rid of the pesky child. Her mammy needed to do a better job of watching her. The child was always showing up out of nowhere with an abundance of questions and insights. Reckon I could only avoid her for so long before she was bound to find me. Over the last months, I'd heeded Miss Rita's words of warning and dodged the child when she came searching.

"What you want to know?" I said.

"Those marks on your back and arms—how did you get them?"

"How you suppose I got dem?" The harshness in my tone didn't seem to discourage the child.

"Your master," she said matter-of-factly. "Papa used to be mean like that, but lately he's nicer to the slaves. Now he is just mean to me." Her lip quivered. "I don't know what I did to make him so mad."

I could tell her what she'd done. The girl was as stubborn as an ornery old mule. She didn't listen to no one. If her pappy told her to stay away from the darkies running his plantation, she was sure to do the opposite.

If he told her to not run, she'd gallop and grin while doing it. The girl had more spirit than a wild horse, and I reckoned Masa Charles was looking to break that willfulness. No one liked an unruly child, but the whites, well, they looked at their children as possessions. A willful child, much like a disobedient wife or slave, reflected poorly on the family and painted an image to society that the man of the family wasn't in control of his household.

"You scoot now and go find dat chile dat follows you 'round lak she your shadow," I said.

Miss Willow's mouth fixed with defiance. "She has a name, you know. It's Mary Grace, and she's my soul sister."

Soul sister? I gawked at the child like she were crazy.

Eyes wide with fear, she bounded forward before I could stop her and grabbed my arm. I froze, unsure what to do. "That just slipped out," she said. "Please don't tell Papa. He'll be awfully cross with me. He says, 'Willow, no colored can be your friend. You're a white girl, and that makes you different.'" She held out her arms. "But you see, mister, I'm not different. Mammy says I'm just like the rest of the coloreds, I was just born to a white mama and papa." She paused as if in thought. "I don't know my mama. She died when I was little. I wish I knew what she was like, but Papa never speaks of her."

I grunted.

"Mammy says I can love Mary Grace like a sister in my heart, just don't be saying it to Papa or anyone else…" She went on and on as I struggled to keep up with her.

It was indisputable the girl cared for the slave child in a way that went beyond the idea that she was a toy plucked from the quarters to entertain the masas' children. Tenderness swelled in the soul of Miss Willow. And her intense protectiveness of Miss Rita's girl bucked against my feelings for her kind.

"Miss Willow!" The shout made Miss Willow and me both jump.

She lowered her voice, ignoring the call. "That's Mammy. If I get caught bothering the slave folk, she'll be furious. Papa says I have to mind Mammy. I don't care so much, except when she doesn't let me come down to the quarters." She shrugged. "But Mary Grace and I sneak down there anyhow. Mammy says she has eyes everywhere." She took a breath. "Mary Grace and I try to get a look at them when she takes her head rag off, but we haven't seen no other eyes besides the two on her face." Confusion over her quest to locate her mammy's all-seeing eyes played on the child's face.

Amused at her dismay, I barked a chuckle. Her head jerked in my direction, and she smiled, real pretty like. "You laugh funny," she said. Her smirk dissolved. "Listen, if you want, mister, we can be friends. It can be our secret. I won't tell no one. Not even Mary Grace."

I collected myself and withdrew from my growing intrigue of the chatty child as her mammy called again. "You bes' be gwine 'fore you git us both in trouble. Your mammy ain't nobody I want to be messing wid."

She bobbed her head and continued. "Don't worry about Mammy none. She's loud and bossy to most folks, but inside she's squishy like—"

"Miss Willow, we got to go before Mama catches you," someone whispered behind us.

I whirled, my heart thumping hard as Mary Grace stepped out from the shadows of the barn. She cast a look over her shoulder as if expecting her mama to slip up on her.

"I got to git back to work." I grabbed my soiled shirt and half ran to get away from the girls.

Safely back in the fields, I found myself thinking on the white child, and again, Magnolia crept into my mind. Oh, how she would talk, asking never-ending questions until my lids grew heavy. And, on this day, my heart smiled at the memory.

CHAPTER
Nine

MASA TOOK ME WITH HIM TO TRADE WITH THE "Croatan" or "free people of color" who lived in cabins along the river. His involvement with the family clan—viewed by the whites as no better than a colored—went beyond him looking to reap a profit. He partook in their traditions, learned their language, and lowered the barrier he forged around himself. It was among these peculiar people that the masa appeared at ease.

Some of the tribespeople were sharecroppers at Livingston, and they resided in the quarters with us. Folks said the land was theirs long before the white settlers moved in and forced them from their lands. Masa said that the colonists enslaved them, exported them through Charles Town harbors to the West Indies, and sent their womenfolk to England and forced them into service in Englishmen's homes. They shipped off the tribespeople in boats to New France in the Province of Canada.

It was in Masa Charles's treatment of these people that I witnessed his fairness and generosity and how he had earned their respect. One day, as I drove the wagon away from the plantation by the river and onward toward Livingston, I pondered on the masa, who sat beside me on the seat writing in a ledger. And, for a brief second, I considered that maybe all white folks weren't made equal.

Above a hawk soared, and I became engrossed in the magnificent spread of his wings. Nature had a way of soothing a man's soul. The lull of the countryside beckoned me, and I found myself looking forward to driving the masa. On several occasions, he engaged in conversations with me in a manner a masa never would a slave; instead, he conversed as I'd seen him do with his lawyer friend and other white folks. It was as if he considered me smart enough to comprehend what he was saying. Maybe, like me, it was the widespread countryside that sang to him. Away from Livingston, he became a different man. The passion I'd seen in his eyes on his ship was alive again, but when Livingston came into view a more solemn, troubled man emerged. And I wondered what it was about the place that haunted him.

Sometimes during our outings, he was deeply immersed in his ledgers and spoke very little. While other times, memories or thoughts would occupy his mind. He'd stare off into the swamps and woods, his expression contorted from his natural reservation to a grimace or a look of yearning. His chest would expand, and he'd let out a long sigh. And whatever weighed down his mind, he managed to shake off.

Today I glanced sideways at the tallies he etched into his records. When he caught me looking, his pencil stilled, and I promptly returned my focus to the road.

"James?"

"Yes, sah."

He hesitated a moment before continuing. "Can you read? Or write?"

I coughed, choking back my shock. Even if I could make sense of the figures on his pages, only a fool would divulge such a truth. My mind leaped to the day by the river and the doings of the little missus. Teaching a slave girl to write—why, it was more than dangerous, it was deadly. If someone had come along and caught them, they'd whip Miss Rita's girl as quick as nothing. Masa Hendricks would be fined or imprisoned. Not to mention what Miss Willow's pappy would do to her if he found out what she'd been up to with Mary Grace.

"Evvybody knows slaves ain't allowed to read or write," I said.

He adjusted himself on the seat to look at me. "You didn't answer my question."

I squirmed under his intense stare. "Ain't had much use for et."

"Would you like to learn?" His question was slow, as if he were considering the madness in what he asked.

My eyes shot to meet his before I lowered my gaze to its rightful place. "W-what you mean?"

"A man can hardly go through life not knowing to what he signs his name."

"Slaves don't have no need to learn. Don't reckon we be signing anything of importance, seeing as we don't have important matters to concern ourselves wid."

"But...I want to know, if situations weren't as they are, would you want to learn how?"

Beads of sweat dampened my brow. What trickery did he speak? "Ain't fitting for a slave," I said.

"Those over there, what are they?" He pointed at the trees lining the stretch of road.

I frowned. "Trees, Masa."

He lifted his hands. Using his index fingers, he formed a cross. "This is the letter *T*. Tree starts with the letter *T*."

T. I marked the stick letter in my mind while observing the trees ahead. Gooseflesh prickled my skin. Slowly I nodded, acknowledging my understanding.

From the corner of my eye, I saw a rare smile cross his face before he held out his ledger for me to see. "See this letter here? It's an *R*. The word 'tree' is spelled with four letters. T, R," he steered me to another marking in the book, "E, and another E. T-R-E-E. Tree." He glided his fingers over the letters, beaming with satisfaction.

My pulse raced. Could the whisperings in the quarters be true? Had Masa Charles—a man profoundly rooted in the ways of the South—been reborn? Did he care for the Negroes like he did the tribesmen by the river? Miss Willow had said that her pappy was a different man than he once was. If so, what had caused such a significant change in him?

Masa quoted the spelling two more times, and I stored it in my head like the word was a ration that would never be offered again. "T-R-E-E," I repeated. Then again. A vast thirst awoke in me. A grin escaped me before my distaste for the whites choked out the twinge of pride stirring in my chest, and I retreated behind the disconnect I'd survived in all these years. I clamped my lips shut.

As if sensing my withdrawal, he cupped my shoulder with a reassuring hand. "You need not worry. This would be our secret, as we both understand the risk if this got out. If you're interested, I'll teach you more." He waited for a reply, but I didn't offer one. Masa Charles had been kinder than my former masas, and more forthcoming than a masa usually was with a slave; however, I wasn't easily fooled. I emptied my mind of weak sentiments. White folks had no care for darkies, beyond what we could or couldn't do for them.

"Knowledge is freedom," Masa said quietly, as though he didn't want the wind to carry his words. "And perhaps it's a step in the deliverance from oppression suffered by the Negroes. We've wronged you. Our crimes upon you are unforgivable. I once employed men who devalued your women as their men stood outside, waiting, helpless to protect them. Your children worked my fields until their fingers bled, and they dropped in exhaustion. I saw no wrong in my actions or those of the South. Until…" His voice hitched. "What if those children had been my daughter?"

I thought of Miss Willow slaving in the fields. And scoffed inwardly. It was hardly a comparison at all, as a wealthy plantation owner's daughter would never be subjected to such hardship. Only in losing everything would his daughter work his lands as my Mag had done at a tender age. Relief from the yokes they placed around our necks was a fool's dream. They would continue to rule this nation, and breed hatred into their offspring while we lay the foundation for them to build their empires. Like the tribesmen, we were a conquered people.

Caught up in my resentments, at first I failed to notice the far-off look Masa got in his eyes.

"All children should live in their innocence," he said. "Not be scarred with the horrors we embed into their young souls and minds. They should be free to play and discover while their youth lasts, not serve their masters from sunup to sundown." Shame washed over his face. "Too many sins stain my hands."

I sat stunned by the revelation of his innermost thoughts. Silence fell like a weight, a rain cloud hovering over us. We rode along, each lost to our own fiends, but when he spoke, I wasn't prepared for the vulnerability I saw in him.

"Do you suppose there's forgiveness for someone like me?" His voice cracked.

"I-I don't know, Masa...I reckon we all got our own wrongs in dis life."

He heaved a sigh. "For far too long, we've controlled the blacks because we were afraid of what you all would become," he said. "My situation, as of late, is different than most. I need you all for more than your skills and labor." His voice dropped to a whisper. "You see, the law prevents me from freeing you all, but behind the curtain of the working slave plantation Livingston appears to be, I need men like you to help me in my quest to make Livingston a refuge for the slaves I can help."

What was he saying? Was he one of those abolitionist people that helped folks like me?

"I'm sure you have seen by now that Livingston is not what it appears to be to outsiders."

I'd seen, all right. The overseer carried a whip, but I'd never seen him use it. Clem had told me it was forbidden. But that warn't the only thing I'd noticed that was off about the place. At Livingston, the slaves were reprimanded as an overseer would be by the masa. No rations were withheld, no lockups took place. Though it was illegal according to the Slave Code to allow blacks to congregate without the presence of whites, Masa allowed his slaves to hold Sunday services in the north barn, led by a black preacher from the quarters, with strict instructions they were to keep the praising down. However, every now and then the amens would rise, and from the blacksmith's shop I'd see the pigeons that nested in the rafters of the barn take flight. Then the overseer would march to the barn and gain control of the worshiping, and all would grow quiet again.

"Can't help but notice," I said.

"Which brings me to another matter," he said. "Willow has brought it to my attention how you care for the horses and, upon her request, I'm removing you from the fields to tend the horses and to continue in the trade you are skilled at. Livingston could use a blacksmith. With Jabet's arthritis acting up, he isn't keeping up to the demands of the plantation. What do you say?"

My stomach fluttered and I cleared the lump lodging in my throat. "Thank you, Masa."

"Maybe selfishly I hope that this will be a stepping stone in building trust between you and me." His honesty in revealing his ploy to mold my opinion of him to his favor, though shocking, helped me feel appreciation for him.

Upon our return to Livingston, I drove the wagon around to the work yard, and Masa Charles climbed down. "See to it the wagon is unloaded, and the supplies stored properly." He tucked his ledger under his arm.

"Straightaway." I inclined my head and lifted the reins to guide the team.

"Until next time, James." A gleam shone in his eyes and, catching his meaning, I tipped my hat.

"Good day," I said and flicked the reins.

With the help of some menfolk, I unloaded the wagon and stored the goods in the warehouse. All the while, I recited in my head, *T-R-E-E*. In my mind's eye, I envisioned my fingers making the cross like Masa's had.

Later, standing in the doorway of the stables after I'd tended to the horses, I glanced over the plantation, and a grin stretched my face and pounding in my chest.

Maybe…Masa Charles's place ain't so bad.

CHAPTER
Ten

MASA CHARLES REMOVED ME FROM THE FIELDS AND gave me the position of farrier and assistant to Jabet. He kept his promise to teach me to read and write and, as an eager student, I learned quickly. At night as I lay on the corn-husk pallet next to Clem, I silently recited the spelling of words. During the day, when Jabet had his back turned, I'd sketch the letters in the soot before dusting away the evidence of Masa's and my secret. Each morning I rose early before the plantation awakened to go to the corral and whisper, freely, my learnings to the horses. And for the first time in years, a spark of hope kindled in me.

The day of the outburst in the big house, Masa had returned from visiting the Widow Jenson's farm.

A stable boy brought the masa's stallion to the stables. "Masa wants to see you up at de big house."

I took the reins and guided the horse to a stall, where I unsaddled him. *H-o-r-s-e*. My mouth moved to form the letters.

"You saying somepin'?" the boy asked.

I looked over the back of the horse at him. "No."

His brow wrinkled and he cocked his head. "Your lips moving, but you ain't talking?"

"Ain't you ever talked to yourself 'fore?" I said gruffly.

He shrugged. "Suppose so."

"You fetch some feed and take care of his horse, and I see what de masa be needing." Leaving him to finish with the horse, I headed for the big house.

As I placed my foot on the bottom step of the gallery, Masa's bellow launched my heart into my throat.

"Enough! You'll learn your place, Olivia!"

Olivia? Had she returned? I'd overhead some womenfolk speaking about Masa's wife—a woman most of them had never known. They'd said Missus Olivia warn't dead at all, but instead she had run off. I'd wondered why Masa and Miss Rita allowed Miss Willow to think she was dead. Maybe as a way of protecting her from the truth, that her mama had abandoned her. Surely that was worse than believing she had died. Folks said Masa's wife had broken his heart when she left him and the girl. And because of this, he'd never been able to move on. But people involving themselves in others' affairs was something I wanted no part of, so I never asked questions and closed my ears to wagging tongues.

Muffled voices came from inside, and I spied the commotion through the library window. Miss Willow stood with her head hanging low, her dark hair concealed beneath a head rag. Her frock of ribbons and fine fabric was gone, and instead she wore a shift that womenfolk and children in the quarters wore.

Miss Rita's hands lifted in a plea. "Masa, please. Miss Willow didn't mean no harm. I thought I bes' tell—"

"Stop defending her!" Masa said. "I fear we're spoiling the child. And you know what's at stake here with her behaving in such a manner." He paced the room, his hands resting on his waist. Then his gaze centered on his daughter. "Willow, for heaven's sake, remove that rag from your head." The child obeyed as he came to stand in front of her. He held out his hand, and she placed the cloth within his grip. "You'll go to your room and stay there until supper. No trays of food are to be taken up to her, do you hear me, Henrietta?" He cast a look at Miss Rita. "And furthermore, keep your daughter away from her."

"Yes, Masa. I do as you say."

"But, Papa," Miss Willow's voice was hoarse from crying, "I'll starve without any food. I—"

"You'll hardly starve," he said, exasperated. "I grow tired of your antics." He lifted his fingers and rubbed his temples. "Why do you set out to defy me?"

"I don't, Papa. I—"

He waved a hand in the air for her to stop. "You blatantly disobey me. No more. This time you'll take your punishment and learn from it. A good paddling is what you need."

"No!" Her wail carried.

I looked around, not sure if I should step inside or wait. When the voices inside lowered, I sat down on the bottom step to wait. It wasn't the first time I'd witnessed Masa unleashing his wrath on the girl. But what had angered him enough to call the girl by her mama's name? The name folks said was banned. Miss Willow was responsible for most of the fallouts she had with her pappy, but today it hit me hard in the gut. I didn't figure the girl meant any harm; she was a child, and children had a way of getting themselves into trouble. Why, my Mag, she—

"Willow, come back here," Masa said as footsteps stomped across the gallery and down the steps beside me.

I jumped to my feet as Miss Willow rushed by in a fit of sobs. A knot stuck in my chest. "I git her, Masa," Miss Rita said, worry in her voice.

"No, let her go," he said. "I'm too weary to deal with her now. Maybe once we've calmed down I can talk to her. Some days...I think I'm doing everything wrong."

"You doing de bes' you can, Masa, and dat is 'bout all anybody can do," she reassured him.

Miss Willow had fled, vanishing entirely. I glanced through the railing at the gardener, hunched over a flowerbed. His eyes never lifted, but his ear was tilted toward the big house. And I was sure the little missus's outburst would be floating through the quarters that evening.

Masa and Miss Rita walked out onto the gallery. "James, what are you doing up here?" he said.

"De boy tole me you wished to see me."

"Ah, yes, I'd forgotten already. Tomorrow I need you and another man to go to the Widow's farm and help her get the last of her crop in. A couple of her slaves have a case of influenza, and she requires help."

"As you say, Masa." I bowed.

Some hours later, as the sun was setting, I heard the masa and Miss Rita out looking for Miss Willow.

"Don't blame de gal, wid how her pappy goes at her sometimes." Jabet stood on the threshold of the blacksmith's shop, watching slaves light and hand out lanterns as they prepared to aid the masa and Miss Rita in their search.

I removed my leather apron and pushed past him, leveling a glare at him. "Don't you think your chatter would be bes' used on finding de gal?" Not waiting for a reply, I jogged across the work yard to Miss Rita's side.

I touched her shoulder. "De gal ain't come back?"

Her pretty, coffee-colored eyes pooled with moisture, and she shook her head. "She runs off from time to time, but never for dis long. We got to find her." She gripped my forearm. "She too young to be out dere alone at night."

"Where do you think she would go?"

"She doesn't lak de dark. I can't see her staying out dis long ef somepin' warn't wrong."

"James." Masa came up behind me.

Annoyance at Miss Willow's pappy sparked inside me as I turned to face him, but the fear in his eyes fizzled my agitation.

"Get a lantern and check down by the river," he said as a stable boy brought his horse. He swung up and reached for a lantern from a slave that stood nearby. "I'll check the perimeter. She couldn't have gone far. You—" he pointed to two younger men "—gather some help and scour the outbuildings."

I didn't wait for him to finish before I grabbed Miss Rita's lantern and took off for the river. The memory of Miss Willow tempting fate by balancing on the edge of the river rushed into my mind, and my feet pounded harder. *Fool gal!* I choked back the fear as my imagination took over.

The rushing sound of the current reached me before I burst through the trees at the end of the trail. "Miss Willie," I called. My voice trembled. I called over and over as I chased the riverbank, searching for her. Each minute that passed, my concern increased. What if she had fallen into the river and the current had swept her away? No, she had been warned about playing by the river. She knew better. I cupped my hand and called louder. "Miss Willie!"

A low cry snatched my breath. "Here."

"Miss Willie! Dat you?"

"Yes."

"Where you be?" I held the lantern higher, squinting into the darkness.

"Over here." Her response came stronger, and I followed her call.

A small figure rested against what appeared to be a towering dark boulder. On closer inspection, I realized it was the boulder I'd found her and Mary Grace reading on some time back.

"Miss Willie." I dropped to the ground and held up the lantern to inspect her. "You all right?"

Her face was puffy with spent tears. She rubbed her eyes to brush the sleepiness from them. Relieved to find her alive, I paid no heed to station; that she was the little missus, and I was a slave. I lifted my hand to remove a twig hanging from her tangled tresses. She leaned into the palm of my hand, seeking consolation. "Is Papa mad?" Fresh tears spilled.

"He skeered," I said, using my thumb to wipe her tears.

"I'm sorry." She began to sob, laying her head against my chest. My heart thumped wildly. "I-I didn't mean to frighten everyone. He'll punish me for sure now."

You and me both. I patted the girl's back, knowing such comfort I offered the white missus was forbidden. "Dere, dere, Miss Willie. Et be all right. Your pappy be more happy to see you unharmed den he be mad." If Masa punished the girl, it wouldn't be without justification. She had the whole plantation in an uproar over her disappearance.

"Come." I drew back. "We need to let de others know you all right."

She brushed back the damp strands of hair sticking to her face. "My ankle, it's hurt. I called for help, but no one could hear me over the noise from the river. I guess I must have fallen asleep. I-I thought I'd die out here, all alone."

I chuckled at the latter part. "You too ornery to die." I handed her the lantern. "You take dis." She obeyed, and I hoisted her into my arms.

As we walked along the trail toward the plantation, I asked, "What you do dis time dat make your pappy so mad?"

"It's Mammy's fault. She told on me," she said in a tone of utter despair.

"What she tell on you for?" I said, knowing Miss Rita wouldn't have snitched on her without good cause.

"Well…" She snuck a peek at me. "I was bored, and I suggested to Mary Grace that we dress up as the field hands and go help in the fields. One of the workers reported us to Mammy, and she came charging after us. Made us sit in the parlor until Papa returned. Sold us out as quick as nothing, she did. I may not forgive her. She says she loves me, but she's always going to Papa and getting me in trouble."

I clucked my tongue at her nonsense. "Miss Rita helps watch over you. And from what I see, I know she cares 'bout you and—"

"But—"

"No buts 'bout et, Miss Willie." I shook my head. "You got to be good to Miss Rita. De same as your pappy. I know he hard sometimes, but he loves you. Et a hard job, being a pappy. So suppose you go a mite easier on dem, and stay out of trouble. Can you do dat for me?" I said as we broke through the trees and the quarters lay before us.

"For you?"

"And for dem." I adjusted my hold on her.

She looked me in the eye. "If you promise to not shoo me away when I want to talk to you, I'll try my very best to do as I'm told."

Well, if she ain't her pappy's daughter! It didn't surprise me she'd offer a proposition of her own. "Dat a promise?"

She bobbed her head and smiled. "I promise with my whole heart."

"Good gal." I gave her a gentle squeeze while wondering how long she'd keep the promise before her obstinacy was bound to emerge. A few days? Maybe a week. The girl was a free spirit, and no matter how much her pappy tried to corral her, she resisted. She was an untamed tigress, and besides the nugget of gold ticking inside of her, it was the trait I admired most 'bout the girl. She wasn't so easily molded into the ways of white society.

As I entered the working yard carrying Miss Willow, cries rose.

"Lard be praised."

"Et Miss Willow. He found her!"

The masa rode into the yard some time later, after a slave had been sent to fetch him. Anguish pulled at his face at the sight of Miss Willow wrapped in a woolen blanket, sitting on the back steps. He dropped from his saddle and raced toward her and, without hesitation, he swept her up in his arms.

"Willow," he groaned, choking on tears. He held the child at arm's length, inspecting her before kissing her forehead and cheeks.

"I'm sorry, Papa. Truly I am…" Her voice quavered. Throwing her arms around his neck, she buried her face and sobbed.

"I'm sorry too, my darling," he whispered into her hair.

Emotions clogged my throat. Then, realizing I was

trespassing on a moment I had no business being part of, I turned and strode toward the stables. Slaves fell away and drifted back inside the big house and down to the quarters. At the doorway of the stables, I looked back as the masa lowered himself on the steps and sat with his daughter on his lap. Some folks may say she was getting too big to be cradled like a little girl, but at this moment the masa gave Miss Willow the love and comfort she needed. He clung to her, the fear of losing her evident in the softness that transformed him. Clearing my throat, I turned away.

I returned later to find them gone. I glanced up at the window I knew to be Miss Willow's bedchamber as the light came on inside. At night when I wanted to be anywhere but in a cabin stocked full of people or pulled into idle chatter around open fires, I'd wander to the corral. It was during these moments that I'd catch Miss Willow, dressed in her nightclothes, sitting at the window, peering down at the quarters. Tonight would prove no different.

Later, when the light went out in her bedchamber, she suddenly appeared at the window with a lantern in hand. This night, she didn't stare in the direction of the quarters; instead, her gaze fastened on me as I stood in the doorway of the stable, my mind occupied with the events of the night. She lifted a hand and waved, pressing her fingers on the windowpane. Cautiously, I returned her wave. Then as suddenly as she'd appeared, she moved away, the lamplight faded, and the room grew dark and still.

I barred the doors of the stable and glanced one last time up at the little missus's window, imagining her tucked in her bed, safe from harm. I unhooked the lantern hanging on the post and as I strolled down to the quarters, warmth rushed through me and like a whisper of the past, my lips parted, and a tune long forgotten emerged.

Fly, my little angel,
Spread your wings and soar
Above the trees may you find freedom,
A slave no more.

CHAPTER
Eleven

A CRISP BREEZE SWAYED THE NAKED TREE BRANCHES that sunny morning in February when I made the discovery in the smokehouse. Earlier that day, I'd been in the carriage house, preparing an open carriage for the masa so he and his girl could attend morning service. Sundays were a day of rest, and the fields and outbuildings lay empty, and an unusual silence enveloped the place. On these days when the plantation folks were preoccupied with Sunday services, I savored the peacefulness of nature's melody void of mindless chatter, meddlesome questions, or curious stares.

"You coming' to mornin' service?" One of the weaver's sons halted in the doorway of the carriage house on his way to the north barn.

I tightened the harness on the Belgian horse. "De Lard ain't got no use for me."

"Preacher says de Lard loves all folkses equal. Even de whites," the boy said.

"Dat be so?" I ground my teeth, weary of such talk. "Dipping in Clem's moonshine, I see," I muttered.

"What dat you say?" he said.

I lifted my head to look over the horse's back. "Don't keep your ma waiting."

"I say a prayer for ya," he said before running off.

You do dat. I climbed up onto the carriage seat, then drove the buggy out the double doors and around the big house to the front yard. I clambered down and hurried to the servant door at the back of the main house, where I asked for a clean blanket to place inside the carriage in case Miss Willow got a chill.

I had barely returned to the front yard and placed the blanket on the seat before Miss Willow bounded down the gallery steps. Wearing a lavender gown, a white cape, and a straw bonnet with long ribbons that matched her dress, she looked angelic.

"Morning, Jimmy," she said, all smiles. On her pappy's orders, she had stopped calling me mister.

I busied myself double-checking the rigging on the horse. "Morning, Miss Willie." I moved along the side of the horse, gliding my hand over its back.

"Will you be joining the other folks for morning service?"

I'd grown accustomed to her nonstop jabbering. "No."

"What you gonna do with yourself with no one around to keep you company?"

"Plan on doing some fishin'," I said.

"Fishing?" Excitement filled her eyes. "If Papa would allow it, I'd come to keep you company."

I bet you would, I mused.

"Last service was a day I wish to forget." She glowered.

"Why dat?"

"For plenty of reasons. To start with, Mr. Carter seated himself next to Papa and me, and not even my handkerchief could block out the smell of garlic and boiled eggs." Her nose crinkled with disgust, and a shudder passed through her. "And Preacher Samuel was so long-winded, Papa elbowed me for letting my eyes droop closed." Her scowl deepened. "Then Mammy was spitting mad when I returned home."

"What for?"

Her dewy cheeks ripened to a pretty cherry shade, long dark lashes brushing over them as she looked down. "Well...I was dreadfully bored and...I used a hairpin to pick most of the lace on my Sunday frock."

A knee-slapping laugh burst from me. "Well, ain't dat somepin'." I shook my head and grinned. "I bet Miss Rita was blowing fire."

A broad grin split Miss Willow's face at my reaction to her predicament last Sunday. Then, staying true to the girl I'd come to know, she hurried on to another subject. "Are you happy here?"

"I reckon et ain't bad," I said.

Perplexed, she regarded me with dismay. "I thought if Papa gave you the task of caring for the horses, you might find some joy in that."

"I mighty grateful you talked to your pappy on my behalf, but you jus' a gal. You can't be worrying 'bout grown folkses' troubles."

"But if you're happy here, then you won't leave," she said anxiously. She fell silent and she heaved a sigh.

"Everyone leaves…except for Mammy and Mary Grace. Papa says I can't say they're practically family, but they are, you know? They're all I've got besides Papa. If something were to happen to him, I wouldn't be alone because I'd have you all."

A wave of tenderness swept through me and I swallowed back the emotions catching in my throat. "Aw, Miss Willie, you be fine. You pappy—"

"Willow, do stop pestering James," Masa Charles said as he strode into the yard.

"Yes, Papa," the child said, her response melodic. But one glance at her revealed the worry hovering over her.

I found myself wanting to lift her melancholy. "She ain't pestering me none, Masa. Miss Willie a fine gal."

Masa gently patted her shoulder as if she was fragile and at risk of breaking. "That she is."

Ducking my head, I moved around the horse to help Miss Willow into the carriage. "I put dat blanket on de seat, in case you git a chill from de breeze kicking up." I pointed at the quilt as her pappy climbed in beside her.

She smiled. "Thank you kindly." She spread the quilt across their laps, taking care to tuck it securely around her pappy.

In those days, Miss Willow's heart yearned to care for him. It was her way of protecting her only blood family. Later I would come to learn that Masa Charles's efforts to keep the secret about the missus's murder and his desire to not repeat the horrors of the past—by saving his daughter from a fate like her mother's —would be the root of the divide between them. Miss Willow's insubordination, her public display of the love she held for the people of Livingston, and the factor she couldn't change—that she was a reminder of the love he'd lost—would become a battleground between them for years to come.

Masa flicked the reins, and the horse trotted down the lane. Miss Willow peeked around the side of the buggy and waved a small, white-gloved hand. I smiled and waved.

Behind me, I heard heavy footfalls. "She got a way of doing dat." Miss Rita came to stand beside me, and we watched the Masa and his girl as they rode out the gates.

"Do what?" I said, never turning to look at her.

"Gitting inside ya." She sighed. "Got a way of wiggling into de tender places you close off."

"Ain't so." I folded my arms across my chest.

"You keep tellin' yourself dat. I know better." She turned and marched back into the big house, only to return moments later with Mary Grace in tow. She cut across the gallery and down the back steps to fall in line with other house folk heading for the north barn.

Later, with a pail of worms and a fishing pole in hand, I caught sight of them as I strode through the working yard on the way to the river. Their eyes skittered around, keeping watch for anybody looking before they slipped into the smokehouse.

With the masa gone and the plantation near lifeless—except for Jones, splayed out asleep in a rocker on his stoop—the thieves figured they'd sneak in and have themselves a feast. Only dimwits would be senseless enough to go thieving from the masa with the overseer resting out in plain sight. All us slave folk knew he slept with one eye open.

As I walked past Jones, he wiggled in his chair and rubbed a hand over his gray-speckled mustache before adjusting the hat blocking the sun from his eyes. My heart beat faster, and I stepped light as I edged past his cabin, not wanting to alert him.

At the smokehouse, I stopped and craned my neck to listen in on the hushed voices coming from inside.

"Mama, I can't run no more. I tired," a child said.

"We ain't got no choice. Eat up. We got to be gwine 'fore dey git back," a woman with a husky voice said.

I heard the shuffling of feet before another woman said, "But we bin running for days, Sara. We sho' to have lost dem. Ain't heard no hounds for a couple days now. I say we take as much of dis food as we can carry and hide out in de swamps. Masa and his men ain't 'bout to go in dere searching."

"No! I'm skeered of de critters dat live in dere," the child said.

"No. We got to keep gwine. Gotta put as much distance as we can between us and dem. My gal is injured and de blood done soaked through dat bandage. Soon et will leave a trail and lead dem right to us," the woman with the husky voice replied.

"De current washed away our scent. Masa's hounds never find us," the other woman said.

"She right, Mama—"

At the crunching of boots on gravel behind me, I spun to find Jones standing almost on top of me. His thick, gray-peppered brows shifted as he looked down his nose at me, then past me. He released a low growl and twisted by me to stride around the side of the smokehouse to the door. My stomach plummeted, and I hurried after him.

He swung the door open. "All right, you best come on out before I come in there and haul you out." His lanky figure filled the doorway, blocking the runaways' escape.

"We comin'. We jus' womanfolkses. Can't hurt ya none."

A child began to whimper.

"Hush, now, Tillie. 'Member what I tole you 'bout being strong?"

The child's weeping grew louder, then became muffled as a woman stepped out into the sunlight with a girl not much older than my Mag was when she was taken away, pulled tight against her side. A younger, thin woman followed behind them. Dirt marred their faces and clothes, and leaves and twigs were stuck in their matted hair.

"Mr. Hendricks doesn't take kindly to folks stealing from him," Jones said.

The older woman's eyes shifted to me. I guessed her to be the one called Sara. In her gaze I read her urgent need to protect her girl. My fingers gripped the pail of worms as I looked from her to Jones. "We hungry, sah. My gal took a fall a few days back. She hurt, and we plumb tired," she said.

"Am I supposed to feel sorry for runaways?" Jones said, his tone even and unchanging. He didn't posture; he seemed to have no interest in instilling fear in the women and child.

"Et being de Lard's day and all, maybe you can find et widin yourself to turn your head, and we go 'bout our way." In the face of adversity, the woman found the courage to stand before the overseer and ask for his mercy.

"I can't do that," Jones said.

My breathing caught. I looked to the girl as she stood silently now, peeking out from her mama's embrace.

"Please, sah. We can't go back dere. Masa threatened to sell my gal from me. Her and Hanna both suppose to go wid a Mr. Hester to Alabama. I never see her 'gain. She all I got in de world." Sobs shattered the mother's words. "I-I beg you, please, let us go. Nobody ever gonna knowed we were here."

My feet edged soundlessly forward; I lifted my pail, ready to strike the overseer down. *Run!* The cry reverberated in my head.

"As I said, I can't do that. And look," he said, pointing to the ground at their feet. I looked to where he gestured. Darkness stained the ground by the child's feet. "Your gal ain't fit to run no more. If your master is looking for you, he'll track you in no time."

"Ef he was gwine to find us, he'da done et by now," the younger woman said boldly. "Sara is smart. Real smart. She bandaged Tillie up and made us cover our scent from de hounds in de river. Den we followed de river at night and still dey ain't found us."

"How long you been running?" Jones said.

Sara swallowed back her fear. "Got to be 'bout a week now."

Jones swerved past the women and into the smokehouse. He soon reappeared with a hunk of salted pork. "Here, get some food into you."

The women and child looked at him warily.

Jones gestured at them with the hand holding the meat. The child inched forward and snatched the offering before returning to hide in the shadows of her mama's skirt.

"James, go fetch them something to drink. We'll figure out what is to be done when Mr. Hendricks returns." He looked back to the women. "Until then, I have no choice but to tie you up."

Jones had me accompany them to the stables and fetch rope. As he bent, binding the child's hands and feet, I held a ladle to Sara's lips. She grasped it within her bound hands, and her keen eyes held mine. My grimace softened. I wanted to reassure the mother that everything would be fine, but I had no assurance that that was the truth. My mind raced. I would go to the masa on their behalf, and plead for his mercy—

The child began to cry.

"Stay calm. Everything isn't as it seems," Jones said, his voice gentler than its usual gruff timbre.

I frowned, eyeing the overseer.

He rose to his feet. "You get on about your day, James. I'll stand watch until the family returns."

I bowed, turned, and walked outside, the

tranquility of the day robbed by the situation in the stables. Helpless to change the fate of the womenfolk and child in the stables, I left them in the hands of the overseer.

✍ CHAPTER ✍
Twelve

DOWN AT THE DOCK, TIME AND THE SERENITY I'D hoped for faded as I sat envisioning what would happen upon the masa's return. First, he'd inquire with his neighbors on whether the runaways belonged to them. If no one claimed them, he'd ride into town and put an advertisement in the newspaper. Notices would be posted on the message boards outside of the general store and others around Charleston. Once word reached their masa, he'd come to collect his property. Then, the child would be sold as their owner proposed.

Under my trembling hand, the fishing pole shook, and the dragonfly perching on the bamboo rod took off. After a while, despondent, I gathered myself and returned to the work yard. Strolling by the stables, I found Jones leaning nonchalantly in the doorway, whittling a stick with his knife.

At the sound of a carriage coming up the lane, Jones straightened. I whirled, my heart beating in my throat. The masa. He was back!

"Alfred has the day off," Jones said, stepping from the shadow of the doorway. "I need you to stand watch."

Callous and carelessly direct, I said, "I ain't no driver, sah." Negro overseers in the position of mastering and snitching on us slave folk? Why, I was no such man. I'd dangle from a rope before I'd stoop so low.

For a brief moment he studied me, something unreadable flickering in his eyes before he closed the distance between us. Placing a hand on my shoulder, he said, "I'm not asking you to betray anyone. They're worse off if they run. I trust you to do what's right."

Jones left me on the threshold, and I watched him meet the carriage and speak to the masa. After a short conversation, the masa's eyes looked past Jones to the barn. He handed the reins to Jones and turned to lift Miss Willow down.

Ever since the discovery of the women and child in the smokehouse, my nerves had me wound tight. I moved away from the entrance, my gut heavy. I couldn't let the women and child go back to their masa. The woman would lose her daughter, and I didn't wish on her the years of heartache and loneliness I'd endured.

Young Willow's sweet face entered my mind, and I swallowed the lump in my throat. I thought on the masa and the goodness he'd shown me. For the first time in my life, I could carry myself with dignity. Each morning when I rose, a sense of pride thumped in my chest.

I stood to lose everything if I helped them.

I looked over my shoulder at the two men, and then at the group huddled in the corner of the clean stall. Agony tore through me as my eyes rested on Tillie. Tears scratched at my eyes. I knew what I must do.

"You gonna make de right choice? Or you gwine to stand dere knowing dey will take my gal from me?" Sara said.

The sharpness of her words pierced my heart. The drumming in my chest increased, but my feet moved forward. I dropped to my knees before them and began to untie the child.

"Thank de Lard, you come to your senses." Sara held out her hands as I scooted over to her.

"Hush," I said, struggling with the ropes, I looked over my shoulder. The men's voices drew near.

"Hurry!" the younger woman, Hanna, cried, her eyes flitting to the doorway.

My body shook with the urgency to get them free. After I'd loosened the ropes on Sara's hands, she pulled them off as I moved on to her feet.

Hanna started to sob. "Please, hurry!"

The knots of the rope around Sara's feet gave way.

"Go. Now! Take your gal and go!" I whispered through gritted teeth, hauling them to their feet.

"We can't leave Hanna," Sara said, panic contorting her face.

"Et her or your gal. You choose." I shook her with such force, her head rocked on her shoulders. "Go!"

Sara looked at Hanna with tears in her eyes. Silently, her mouth moved with the words *I sorry*.

Sobs racked the young woman, and her lips parted, releasing a low, guttural wail. "Go! Save your gal!"

Sara lifted Tillie onto her hip. I took the mother's arm, and we bolted for the back door of the stables. I threw the door open and shoved them through the door. "Run!" I grunted. Her eyes filled with terror, she whirled and ran. I closed the door and rushed back to Hanna, but froze outside the stall at the sound of footsteps entering the stable.

I looked at her. A vast ache hammered in my chest. Echoing her friend's last words, I breathed aloud, "I sorry."

She nodded and dropped her gaze. "Dey free. Dat all dat matters," she said softly. Wrapping her arms around herself, she rubbed at an invisible chill.

"James?" I heard bewilderment in Masa Charles's voice. He stood a few feet away.

I turned to face him. Hanging my head, I awaited the reprimand and punishment that was certain to come. "I sorry, Masa Charles. But I couldn't let you turn dem in." My gaze fastened to the straw beneath his boots. My voice fractured. "I ain't seed my gal in so many years, I forgit what she luks lak."

A deep rumble came from the masa's chest. "Jones said the girl was injured. They can't survive out there on their own."

Jones. Where was he? I looked around. Fear squeezed my throat. My eyes settled on the masa's face.

"I sent him after them," he said knowingly. "We saw you let them out the back door."

"Please, Masa. Don't turn dem in. A child needs her family. And dat li'l gal, she trembles in her own skin. She won't make et widout her mama."

His expression firm, the masa strode into the stall

and crouched beside Hanna. Her eyes large with fright, she scurried into the far corner. "You need not fear. I will not harm you. Livingston is a haven for weary souls like your friends and you." He unknotted her feet before moving on to her hands. "Come." He held out a hand and his gloved fingers unrolled as he offered her assistance.

Hanna used the cuff of her sleeve to wipe her tears, and her whimpering ceased. She glanced up at me, her eyes asking, could she trust him? Slowly, I inclined my head. She hesitantly planted her hand in his. With a thin smile of reassurance, the masa helped her to her feet.

We all shifted as Jones returned with Sara and Tillie in tow.

"Jones, I will leave you to discuss with the women what I proposed to you. Find out where they came from and we'll go from there," Masa said.

Jones nodded.

Masa turned back to me. "James, walk with me."

We left the stables, walking in silence. I trailed behind him. He sauntered along until we were in the middle of a fallow field, where no one but the birds of the sky could hear us. He came to a stop, and I halted in his shadow.

"Come face me, man to man," he said.

I obliged and stood with my head bowed and my hands clasped in front of me.

"A man looks me in the eyes."

"But I a slave, Masa."

"Well then, as my slave, I order you to look me in

the eye!" he said with the underlying bite I had come to relate to the masa.

I lifted my gaze.

"At Livingston, you're a slave by paper alone."

I frowned at his statement, searching his eyes for some sort of clarification.

The look he returned was earnest. "When your old masa and I made a bargain on the road that day, I instructed him to relay a message to Captain Gillies. Do you recall the message?"

Often, I'd pondered on those words and what they meant between the masa and his captain. "Yes, sah. You said, 'Change has come.'"

"Correct. And on the deck of my ship, I offered you a proposition. During that conversation, I told you I'd treat you with fairness. My question to you is, have I abided by this promise?"

"I reckon so."

Taking his time, he untied the tan cravat around his neck. Before unbuttoning the top button of his shirt, he removed his coat and draped it over his arm. "I do not wish to keep you enslaved, but the laws forbid me from setting you free. However, I have resources that I can use to try to get you to freedom. Of course, the final decision I leave in your hands."

My blood raced. "My hands, Masa?"

"Yes. Soon I will leave for England for a few months. Jones and his men will manage Livingston in my absence. I need men like you to help me run Livingston."

"Whatcha mean by *run*?"

"I require ears and eyes to be alert to every person that comes through those gates." He nodded toward the lane in the distance. "You see, James, Livingston isn't as it once was. I don't have it all figured out yet, but I aspire to make it a place where people like you can find some sort of freedom in the South. Nothing will change the fact that enslaved people are in bondage at this place. My hands are tied. But laws or no laws, it's my mission to do what I can for you all. People have a choice to leave or to stay. If you run, I have no choice but to come after you. I cannot chance being found out for not reporting a runaway. The townsfolk would question me on my reasoning. In the past months, I've been able to help slaves along their journey to freedom. Every precaution must be used if I am to continue what I've started. I asked you to trust me on the ship that day, and I'm asking you again."

A strange lightness enveloped me. "So, et be true. You reborn?"

A laugh burst from him. "How I wish that were the case." Sadness washed away the laughter as quickly as it had arrived. "Perhaps then I could start fresh. But we don't get that opportunity in life, do we?"

"No, sah," I said, my shoulders slumped. "All a man can do is take each day as et comes."

"With the intention of making up for past failures?"

"Dat one way to luk at et."

"A man with the wisdom that you possess at my side would be a great asset."

"What you meaning, Masa?"

"I want you to remain at Livingston and join our cause," he said.

"Cause, Masa?" My pulse pounded in my ears.

"Help me to help those enslaved in securing a different kind of freedom."

I considered his proposal. I didn't have anything in life worth fighting for because the one purpose I had was likely dead.

"Lately, I've come to believe that maybe you could help me with a more delicate matter," he said.

"What dat?"

"Willow."

I shuffled my feet in the dirt. "How I suppose to help wid da gal?"

"My daughter's well-being is of the utmost importance to me—"

My flesh prickled as anxiety rose. "Excuse me, Masa, but you must know I'd never hurt de gal. She always leaping out of nowhere, and I jus'—"

He held up a hand. "No need to stress, James. I'm well aware of my daughter's persistence. You mentioned your girl and that you lost her."

"Yes, sah."

"Was she sold?" he said.

"Et bin over ten years now." The pain of our separation was alive in my soul.

Masa dropped his head, and kicked at the untilled earth with the tip of his boot. "It grieves me to hear that. I'm afraid you know as well as I that when folks are sold, tracking them down is next to impossible."

"My gal gone. I know dat." I stifled a sob.

The masa grappled with what to say next as the weight of my loss settled between us. "With my obligations in England, I expect to be gone a few months, and again I leave my daughter in the hands of the folks here. Willow has the heart of her mother, which holds as much good as it does harm. She's too young to understand that her expressions of love and equality in respect to the Negroes is dangerous and must be concealed from those who would seek to harm the child or me. Henrietta has been a godsend, and my daughter has blossomed under her care." He arched a brow. "Though I do wonder what ideas the woman puts in her head, I will not take the only mother Willow has ever known from her. That brings me to my next question. I have a request for you."

"Me, sah?"

He lowered his head, and his voice grew thick. "I am a selfish man. In my weakness, I fear I've wronged my daughter." He lifted his head. "Perhaps, in my request of you, my daughter will not judge me so harshly in years to come." He paused and inhaled deeply, pain shining in his eyes. "I see how Willow has taken to you. And I've noticed how you seem to find amusement in her chatter."

"You done a good job, Masa. She a bright gal," I said wholeheartedly.

"Stubborn. Rebellious. But yes, bright. However, I worry Willow will be her own stumbling block in life." His eyes assumed a far-off look, as though he saw the future splayed out before him. "I fear her passion and her desire to do good will endanger her. Until she comes to understand that what I've done is for her well-being, she'll continue to challenge me. Perhaps she sees through me, and that's why she defies me so. I love the girl as I loved her mother." He focused on me, his hand gently resting on my shoulder. "I need you to protect her. There are those out there who wish to bring harm upon this place. In my absence, I need to know she's safe. Though I have no right to ask this from you."

Harm Miss Willow? A cold knot formed in my stomach. "What you asking of me?"

The masa's intense gaze softened. "That you bestow on Willow the fatherly devotion I see in you." His eyes beseeched me.

I swallowed hard. Me? Father a white gal? Why, it was ludicrous.

"I'll leave you to think about it. I hope that you can give me your answer before I leave for England." With that, he patted my shoulder, walked past me, and strode back toward the big house.

Left standing in the middle of the field, I considered the masa's offer. The same protectiveness that swelled in Miss Willow for Mary Grace the day by the river quickened within me for the white child. I didn't want harm to befall Miss Willow or her pappy.

The giggles of children at play drew my gaze to Miss Willow as she dashed down the back steps of the gallery with Mary Grace hurrying to catch up.

"Hurry, Mary Grace, the Romans are coming! We must defend our castle." Her excitement carried.

I smiled. Goodness lay in Miss Willow, and hope rose in me that she would carry on her pappy's mission.

In the days that followed, I gave Masa Charles my answer, and my years at Livingston became ones of purpose. I came to love Miss Willow with a fierceness much like her pappy's. The privilege to love and care for Miss Willow was the greatest gift a person had ever given me because in her…my Magnolia lived.

Masa Charles and I formed a friendship that held fast through the years leading up to his death. However, although I'd been his confidant, he never revealed to me the secrets that tore at his soul. It was upon his death that I realized the heavy burden he'd carried and the greatness of his love for his wife and Miss Willow.

Like the masa, I had a proposition, and it was one I offered to the Almighty. I offered him a truce. I promised to cease the attempts to end my own life and, in return, I asked that He allow me to stay on at Livingston, as the protector of Miss Willow and a soldier in our mighty cause.

REVIEW NOTE

If you have enjoyed my work, please leave a review on Goodreads, or the platform you purchased the books from. Your reviews are crucial in spreading the word about my books, and I am sincerely grateful for this support from readers.

COMING SOON:

A WHISPER OF WAR

BOOK THREE

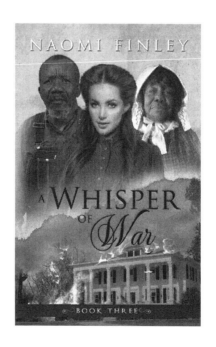

ABOUT
the Author

Naomi is a bestselling and award-winning author living in Northern Alberta. She loves to travel and her suitcase is always on standby awaiting her next adventure. Naomi's affinity for the Deep South and its history was cultivated during her childhood living in a Tennessee plantation house with six sisters. Her fascination with history and the resiliency of the human spirit to overcome obstacles are major inspirations for her writing and she is passionately devoted to creativity. In addition to writing fiction, her interests include interior design, cooking new recipes, and hosting dinner parties. Naomi is married to her high school sweetheart and she has two teenage children and a dog named Egypt.

Sign up for my newsletter: authornaomifinley.com/contact

Printed in Great Britain
by Amazon